GW00392083

The Heart and Soul of Olney

First Published 2004
Published by Lewis Kitchener

Printed in Great Britain by
Avalon Print Ltd
Heathfield Way
Kings Heath
Northampton
NN5 7QP

Dedicated to my husband and daughter
with much love.

"Now stir the fire, and close the shutters fast,
Let fall the curtains, wheel the sofa round,
And, while the bubbling and loud hissing urn
Throws up a steamy column, and the cups,
That cheer but not inebriate, wait on each,
So let us welcome peaceful ev'ning in".

William Cowper

Acknowledgments and Thanks

Thank you just doesn't seem enough, or the right words, for all of the support and help I have received whilst writing this book. To the Olney and Emberton Community Workers, thank you all so much for the co-operation and support you have given me in compiling this chapter, your patience is greatly appreciated.

And to those that helped me the most, and, who's choice it is to remain anonymous, (and they know who they are) **Thank you!**

I really am truly indebted to you all for all you have done it's been an absolute pleasure, the memories of which I shall treasure forever.

Amazing Grace

Amazing grace! How sweet the sound
That saved a wretch like me!
I once was lost, but now am found,
Was blind, but now I see.

'Twas grace that taught my heart to fear,
And grace my fears relieved;
How precious did that grace appear
The hour I first believed.

Through many dangers, toils and snares,
I have already come;
'Tis grace hath brought me safe thus far,
And grace will lead me home.

The lord has promised good to me
His word my hope secures;
He will my shield and portion be,
As long as life endures.

Yes, when this flesh and heart shall fail,
And mortal life will cease,
I shall possess, within the veil,
A life of joy and peace.

Th earth shall soon dissolve like snow,
The sun forbear to shine;
But God, who called me here below,
Will be forever mine.

John Newton

Contents

Olney Bridge c.1821 Courtesy of the Cowper and Newton Museum, Olney.

Welcome
Olney to

Welcome to Olney!

We have much to offer here in Olney and I hope that visitors will enjoy discovering it all, and that residents will do more exploring to discover previously unknown parts of the Town. Olney is very proud of its successful track record in the Thames and Chilterns Britain in Bloom and the Bucks Best Kept Village competitions. It has also received a Highly Commended award for community involvement and has again won the prestigious National Britain in Bloom competition for 2003.

Olney has many excellent pubs and eating-places specialising in food from different countries. Sport plays a big part in the Town and Olney boasts some of the best pitches in the County and many clubs thrive here. The children are also well catered for with several play areas throughout the Town.

We are virtually self sufficient for shopping and the Town is particularly noted for antiques. A few of the traditional family owned shops still close on a Wednesday afternoon but there is a flourishing general market every Thursday in the Market Place. Various events occur throughout the year in Olney, among which is the famous Pancake Race; Floral Fiesta Week in July, which includes a Grand Parade; a large Bonfire and Firework display; and a Dickens of a Christmas celebration, which is normally held on the second Sunday in December.

Olney has grown extensively in recent years and the Town is still expanding, both at the southern and northern ends. There are also some very peaceful spots to enjoy a little tranquillity, including Cherry Orchard, which is situated by the cemetery.

So, come and have a good day out, browse around, visit our Museum, pick a restaurant or a pub for lunch and then sit back and relax on one of the many benches in the Market Place and watch the world go by!

Barbara Smith
The late Town Mayor of Olney 2002- 2003

Britain in Bloom

Buckinghamshire has many gardens, large and small; public parks and private window boxes.

Regrettably many gardens hide behind high walls and hedges where they can't be seen.

If you have ever shown a visitor the plants in your own garden,

Then you will know the pleasure and pride, which your Council aims to encourage.

Advantages in bright and tidy gardens are more pleasant and colourful surroundings, with less weeds; and

If your neighbours see the show that you can provide, they may be shamed or inspired to action.

Nobody can claim that there isn't some area which could not be made more attractive with a splash of living colour; window boxes at the front? The office window? The shop front? The school buildings?

It is the Council's aim to keep the public parks and buildings looking attractive; it is every individual's responsibility to make the community pleasant to live in and to look at.

Now is the time to plan to help the Council win the National Trophy.

British Travel, the National Tourist Organisation, offers special prizes to individuals in the place that wins the trophy.

Large cities with natural resources and funds will have no advantage over industrial towns, nor will picturesque villages. The trophy is awarded for actual achievement, so everyone starts equal.

Official support is given to the campaign by your Council which, among other things, will provide flowers, shrubs and trees in public places.

Outside the Council's sphere is where the public can help - in every garden, window box, hospital, filling station, school or shop.

Millions of visitors come to Britain every year and some no doubt will pass your own premises. First impressions matter very much, bright flowers and tended gardens can be very welcoming to the stranger.

Olney: Winners of the Britain in Bloom Competition
1992,1995,1996,1997,1998,1999,2000,2001

Olney: Winners of the Best Kept Village Competition
1985,1993,1994,1999,2001

3

Olney in General

No one is quite sure where the name Olney originated from, but it is known to date back as far as Anglo Saxon times. Olney was also mentioned in the Treaty of Wedmore 876AD, a time when the land was in the hands of the Danes.

The name could have originated from a couple of possibilities. "Aln-ey", signifys the island of alder trees; or from a Saxon King named Ola, who was reputed to have owned the land at one time. The syllables "ey" or "eye" denote a watery place, which is exactly what Olney is.

Spelling Olney

These are just a few of the ways Olney has been spelt over the years:

10th Century	Ollaneg
11th Century	Olnei (as recorded in the Domesday Book)
12th Century	Olnea
13th Century	Ounela, Ouneya
13th-15th Century	Olneye
16th Century	Alney
18th Century	Olney

Other spellings recorded through time have been:

Oulny
Wolney
Oulney

Olney's Lingo

Many often ask, " What is the correct way to pronounce Olney? " Well, like the spelling, the local dialect has also changed over the years so there is no hard and fast rule as to the correct pronunciation. However, today, those who have lived here for some time generally pronounce Olney, Oney; but newcomers and those who are unsure tend to say Ol-ney. The same idiosyncrasy pops up with pronouncing William Cowper's name. Some say Coo-per, others say Cow- per but at the end of the day, either is accepted, with no right or wrong answer (which is just so typical of Olney).

Olney's Size

Olney, including the Parish of Warrington, is 4 miles long, 2.5 miles wide and has 3410 acres with a population today of nearly 6,500.

Year	Population
1801	2003
1811	2268
1821	2339
1831	2334
1841	2362
1851	2265
1861	2284
1871	2672
1881	2362
1891	2409
1901	2705
1911	2871
1921	2651
1931	2438
n/a	
1951	2337
1961	2384
1971	3603
1981	4375
1991	4929
2001	5367

Population Chart of Olney 1801 - 2001

Not The Only Olney

Did you know that Olney is not alone? In fact there are quite a few of them scattered worldwide with more just waiting to be discovered. The following are just a few of the Olney's that have been found so far.

1. Maryland
2. Texas
3. Illinois
4. Philadelphia
5. Oregon
6. Alabama
7. Georgia
8. Kentucky
9. Missouri
10. Montana
11. Oklahoma
12. Northamptonshire
13. Buckinghamshire

The White squirrel of Illinois.

Olney's Coat of Arms

The origin of a Coat of Arms and Crests, and when and why they became popular, is unknown. There are theories that date them back to the time when the feudal Knights of the Realm used a highly decorated shield to defend themselves during battle. Over time, the shields were decorated with various quarterings and they ultimately became a specific symbol for either a family or a town. There are two variations of Olney's Coat of Arms, the oldest and most typically used one dates back to 1572.

The 1572 Coat of Arms

In 1907, book publisher and local author Oliver Ratcliff set out on a personal mission to find out if Olney had ever owned or possessed its own official Coat of Arms. Regardless of whom he asked, no positive answer was forthcoming; nobody seemed to know, which Oliver thought was very strange considering the Town's past history and connections. Eventually, whilst researching the Antiquities of the Newport Hundreds, Oliver found his first clue.

Oliver's research took him to Weston Underwood and to the grave of Sir Robert Hungerford who had been a well-respected resident of the Village. Whilst clearing the grave, a brass plaque with an engraving of a Coat of Arms came into view and he soon realised this was indeed the Coat of Arms that he had been look- *Olney's Coat of Arms.*
ing for.

History then goes on to tell us that after Sir Robert Hungerford died, his widow,

Elizabeth, went on to marry a Throckmorton, another well to do and respected family in Weston Underwood at the time. When Elizabeth died, the Coat of Arms was updated to include her current families' quarterings, which were later added to her grave plate. With renewed interest in the Coat of Arms and its association, the remaining family gave permission for Olney to use the Coat of Arms as its own, which it did until 1977.

The 1977 Coat of Arms

In 1977 and in commemoration of Queen Elizabeth's Silver Jubilee, Olney's Town Council decided to update the existing Coat of Arms. Various artists submitted their drawings and designs but local artist and author, C. R. Perkins, was the winning contributor.

The new design incorporated many of the original features, as well as some new ones. The Buckinghamshire Swan was added and the roundels were replaced with crescents, and symbols representing Olney's past boot and shoe trade connections were also included. Lace and agriculture elements were also incorporated into the crest and new references to William Cowper, John Newton and Henry Gauntlett were added. Finally, the Latin inscription, " Fove Prisca, Postera Tuere" was added which, when translated aptly means;

" CHERISH THE PAST, ENHANCE THE FUTURE".

Elements of Olney's Town Crest

Shape: Its shield-like shape means defender
Colour: Background is a purple, which reflects sovereignty and justice
Crosses: Symbolic of a Christian experience or sentiment
Embattled Line: This broad and black band represents the walls of a fortress or town
Gold Roundels or Crescents: One who has been found worthy of trust and treasure

Historic Olney

Jurassic Olney

170 million years ago and at a time when the climate was sub-tropical, Ceitiosaurus Oxonenisis roamed in the fields of Clifton Hills, Olney. Ceitiosaurus, whose name means Whale Lizard, was a sauropod, which measured 15 meters long and weighed 30.5 tonnes. It had a whip-like tail, a long neck and a very small head. Ceitiosaurus was vegetarian by nature and would probably have lived in a herd that spent its time lazily roaming the area, munching on the vegetation from the tops of the trees.

Ceitiosaurus Oxenius.　　　The remains of a Ceitiosaurus were found in a field near the Robin Hood Public House in Clifton Reynes just before the first World War, and some of the findings are now on display in the Gordon Osborn Room, Cowper and Newton Museum, Olney.

Roman Olney

"1/4 mile north of the bend of the Ouse and on the line of a possible Roman road parts of a Roman building is still visible. From the neighbourhood came a hoard of silver coins of c3-4 date and a bronze figure of Mercury as well as a contemporary "terra sigillata" and coarse wares".
Sir Nikolaus Pevsner, 1960.

There has been much recorded past evidence of Roman Occupation in and around Olney and on the high grounds of Clifton Hills and across the river to the east a bit, early traces of man have been found.

In 1908 the rector of Clifton Reynes, the Reverend C.W. Fuller, described how workmen who had been working in a nearby quarry had become puzzled by the large quantity of what seemed like underground dwellings they were uncovering. These large pits had been filled with surface soil, rubbish and animals bones. So the work was halted and the British Museum was contacted. The British Museum sent out Reginald Smith F.S.A to investigate who

A typical Roman solider.

later confirmed that the site was indeed of historical interest, as the uncovered remains proved to be that of a very early British underground village.

A bit closer to home and at the northerly end of Olney stands a field known locally as **Ash Furlong**. In this field a Roman Tax Office once stood and it was here that the local landowners went to pay their taxes. It also happens to be in the same vicinity where the original Roman road was and, being at the top of the hill, the station could be easily defended and guarded should it ever have be attacked; as, the area was predominately dense woodland at that time.

Numerous Roman coins dating back to the reign of Constantine were found at the site, as well as a small bronze statue of Mercury, which was given to the local landowner at the time. The findings from the site led to a public exhibition in the Town, but there is no record of their whereabouts after that.

The Romans eventually abandoned the Station, and, over time the building fell into disrepair and disintegrated. The area has since been re-developed and new houses have been built. However, prior to the re-development, older residents of the Town can still recall the field with a building on it.

Notable Roman finds

Limestone Carving of Mercury

A limestone carving of the god Mercury was found by the late Gordon Osborn at the Emberton Gravel Pits, or as they are better known today as, Emberton Park. This small carving was thought to have been produced locally and used as a household shrine.

This carved figure of Mercury was considered a symbol of commercial transactions as he wears a winged hat, and in his left hand he holds a caduceus (a herald's wand); and in his right hand he holds a bag of money. When the carving was found it was damaged in one corner, which is no doubt the result of what happens when something is thrown down a well as part of a sacrifice. The artefact is now on display at the Buckinghamshire County Museum, Aylesbury.

A lime stone carving of the god Mercury.

Samian Pottery

This fine Roman tableware was made on the Greek island of Samos – hence the name Samian – and found its way on to our ancestors' dining tables here in Olney. The pottery has a slip-coated glossy surface and was obviously much sought after in its time as vast quantities were shipped in to Britain after the Roman Invasion of 43 AD. Examples of this pottery and other finds from the local area can be found in the Gordon Osborn Room at the Cowper and Newton Museum, Olney.

Olney and the Domesday Book

In 1085 the Christmas Court of King William carried out the first ever land survey of England. Prior to this survey there had been numerous disputes between landowners throughout England who were unhappy with the amount of taxes they were being made to pay. So the King decided to resolve the matter quickly and fairly and sent out his Royal Commissioners to every County in England with an extensive list of questions that he wanted answering. Sadly the King died before the survey was finished but the findings went on to be recorded as the No.1 document in the Public Records Office, or as it is better known today, the Domesday Book.

This is what the King's Commissioners had to say about Olney,

The Bishop of Coutances holds Olnei to himself.
It answers to 10 Hides
Land for 10 ploughs
3 Hides: 3 ploughs there
24 Villagers with 5 smallholders and have 7 ploughs
5 Slaves
1 Mill at 40's and 200 eels;
Meadow for 10 ploughs:
Woodland, 400 pigs
In Total, Value £12
When acquired, £7
Before 1066, £12

Burgred held this manor; 1 Freeman his man had 1.5 virgates he could sell.

understanding the entry

Size of a Virgate

A virgate is an early English measurement of land, which varies between 15,20,24,30 or even 40 acres. The size of a virgate can vary in different regions throughout England.

Size of a Hide

Another early English measurement of land - originally about 120 acres - which was considered large enough to support a family.

The Woodland

The Woodland referred to in the entry is known to have been Yardley Chase.

The Mill

The 1086 Mill, as it was referred to, was thought to have stood somewhere at the foot of Clifton Hills, Olney. There is much evidence to support a mill being there, although a mystery still remains to this day as to its exact location. And, to add to this, numerous mills are recorded for this area so it makes it very difficult to determine which Mill was actually the Domesday Mill.

The Eels

As for the eels, these were very popular and plentiful in 1086 and still are today, if you know where to look.

An early engraving of Olney's Market Place, c.1850 Cowper and Newton Museum, Olney.

The Market Place

The Market Place

Records of a market being held in Olney can be dated as far back as 1205. Traditionally the market sold both livestock and fresh produce and was held once a week, on a Monday. However, by 1800, the law had changed and the market became fortnightly and held on a Thursday.

Commemorating the coronation of King George and Queen Mary, Market Place Olney c.1911, Cowper and Newton Museum, Olney.

Livestock was sold from a large building that once stood on a site behind the Museum and the fresh produce was traded from stalls on the Market Place. During its lifetime the Cattle Market became a grading centre for the Government but this arrangement came to an end when rationing ceased in 1954.

Then in March 1987, the last moos and bleats were heard and the Cattle Market closed after 600 years of trading. It was claimed that the changes in the social climate and urban trends were the main causes of the closure.

The Farmers Market

On Sunday 7th September 2003, after 16 years of being dormant, Olney's Farmers Market was revived and has been held ever since on the first Sunday of each month from 10.00am to 2.00pm. This Market concentrates on local produce – no livestock this time- and the producers must be local, i.e., from within a 30 mile radius of Olney. Also, each stall must be run either by the producer's family or by an employee directly involved with its production.

Olney's Farmers Market.

The Farmer's Market has proved to be highly popular, especially with the Town's residents. Which is an indication that these delicious fresh homegrown foodstuffs, nurtured in our local area, are also the preferred choice to those offered in most supermarkets. It's worth rising earlier on those Sunday mornings to buy the mouth-watering ingredients for a full English breakfast, but don't be late; much of the produce is

Olney Market place, c.1900

sold out well before closing time. The main weekly market is still held on a Thursday and consists of a variety of stalls and its is obvious from the traffic in the Town – both pedestrian and vehicular – that Thursday is the most popular day of the week for shopping. As well as being used for the weekly market, the Market Place is also the main car park for the Town, except for Thursdays of course; and it is also used as the focus for other events, such as the Pancake Race and Dickens of a Christmas.

The "Old" Market Place

As with any town, village or city, change and re-development are inevitable for its survival. But next time you cross the Market Place, pause and give some thought to its historic and colourful past, and try and picture the different kinds of hustle and bustle it has seen over the centuries.

Public Punishment

In bygone years, crime and disorder in Olney were dealt with very severely – and on the spot. There were a number of punishment options readily available in the Town, such as the Whipping Post and Public Stocks, which were sited opposite the Cowper and Newton Museum on the Market Place. Then there was cart- tailing - a method of punishment whereby offenders had their hands tied to the back of a cart and were flogged whilst being forced to walk down the High Street to the High Arch, near the Congregational Church. For the ultimate punishment there was the gallows, which were sited at the Warrington Roundabout on the road to Wellingborough.

The Gallows

It was here that body of John Marston is reputed to have been buried. John Marston committed suicide at the Saracens Head Public House, which is now a private house next door to the Bull on the Market Place. The Church, who frowned upon suicides, refused to allow poor John to be buried in sacred ground and therefore, in keeping with local custom at that time, the body was taken to the crossroads at Warrington where it was nailed to a cross and left there as a deterrent to others.

Sheil Hall 1816

(Sheil: Scottish term for shelter)
Sheil Hall was a small but cleverly designed building that stood on the Market Place, roughly where the bus shelter and public toilets now stand. At the front of the build-

ing there was a blacksmith's, which was in a perfect position for catching Olney's passing trade. The remainder of the building was used as a meeting place and according to the diaries of Samuel Teedon (a schoolmaster of Olney), also a school. It has not been possible to determine who built Sheil Hall – and when - but it is known that the entrance to the meeting room / school had a double flight of stairs leading up to an entrance which had bow-fronted windows either side of the doorway and were fitted with glass of an ornate design. The building was demolished in 1816 but for what reason, and by whom, nobody knows.

An early engraving of the Market Place, Round House left, Sheil Hall Right.

The Round House 1846

The Round House was a small hexagonal building, which stood on the Market Place in the vicinity of the current War Memorial. It was known locally as the Town Lock- Up as well as the Round House and it was here that the unruly or the lawbreakers were incarcerated. Like Sheil Hall, there is no recorded evidence as to when the Round House was built, or by whom. Although it is known that it was taken down around 1846 and re-sited further up the High Street by the present Library. The stone ball from the top of the building did survive and has now been given a home in the garden of the Cowper and Newton Museum Olney.

The Pepper Pot Jail, Castle Carey.

There are only five known survivors of these types of lock-ups in England today and one similar to the one Olney would have had can be found in Castle Carey, Somerset - The Pepper Pot Jail, Castle Carey.

The Parish Pump.

The Parish Pump

In 1782 Daniel Raban, a local Baker, paid for the Market Place to be re-levelled and re-surfaced at his own expense. At the same time the work was being undertaken, it was decided to install a water pump for the residents of Olney. This would allow readily available fresh water on demand, as clean water in Olney at that time was a scarce commodity. The Parish Pump, as it became known, is no longer used today but is on display in the back garden of the Cowper and Newton Museum.

The Trees

The trees were planted on the Market place to commemorate the union of the three kingdoms in the reign of James 1st (1625-1640). But over time these three trees grew to an enormous size and eventually succumbed to the ravages of the weather. On the 4th July 1832 the last of the trees came down during a bad storm and, to compensate for the loss, seven lindens were planted in their place.

The Market Place in brief

Olney's Market Place is host to many fine, unusual and quaint properties. Each one is different, unique and, like many things in Olney, probably packed full of history, secrets, unexpected surprises and stories. The next time you are wandering past or going into one of these treasured buildings, try to imagine some of those secrets and stories and what the shoppers of, say 200 years ago would have been wearing. Allen's of Olney is one such place that still oozes with this bygone atmosphere, and is a classic example of time standing still, apart from the prices that is!

Some Classic Examples

No .1 Market Place: Olney Galleries
Grocery Business, 1840.
Tallow Chandler and Wood Dealer.
Furniture Manufacturers: Stanley Woods.
Now: Antique Shop

No. 5 and 6 Market Place: Allen's of Olney
The Bell Public House.
Undertaking services.
Draper's and Milliner's.
Now: Gentleman's Clothes Shop

No. 10 Market Place: Gift Shop
Barbers and Wig Dressers, William Cowper's Barber!
Watchmakers.
Now: Gift Shop

No.12 Market Place (Baptist Chapel Entrance)
The last business that was run from this double-fronted property was a bookshop and stationer's. The Hipwell family purchased and demolished the building in order to build an annexe on to their house Westlands, which is next door. Once the annexe had been built, the remainder of the land was given to the Chapel who constructed the entrance that you see today.

Pancake Day 2003. Courtesy of The Milton Keynes Citizen.

Today's Events

The Olney Pancake Race

Celebrating the Pancake Race in Olney is a tradition that dates back as far as 1445, although the Race has not been run every year since then. This popular and well-attended event is held on Shrove Tuesday, the day when Christians in bygone days cleared out their larders before beginning the Lenten fast the following day, Ash Wednesday.

Canon Collins demonstrating how to toss your pancake.

The Legend behind the Race

The Olney Race is based on an old medieval tale. A housewife in the Town was in her kitchen making her pancakes on Shrove Tuesday when she heard the Church bell ringing for the Shriving Service. Desperate not to be late, she made a mad dash for the Church with her frying pan still in her hand.

Another is told of the local ladies who made the pancakes for the Church bell-ringers, bribing them with these mouth-watering delicacies to ring the Shriving Bell earlier in order to hasten the start of the Shrove Tuesday festivities.

Recent Changes

The Race had lapsed for some years but after the 2nd World War, it was re-introduced by the newly appointed Vicar of Olney, the Reverend Canon Ronald Collins. Whilst clearing out a vestry cupboard he came across some old photographs of the race from the 1920s and 30s. He was so filled with enthusiasm, he called for volunteers to revive the ancient custom and was delighted when 13 ladies agreed and Nellie Bosworth went on to win the first race in 1948.

RJ and Virginia Leete (USA) and Edwin Horlock (Olney) unveilling the Pancake Plaque, Olney Centre.

The Link with U.S.A

By 1950, news of the Pancake Race had spread across the Atlantic to the Town of Liberal in Kansas, U.S.A. liking what they had read they decided to adopt the tradition for themselves and in doing so they challenged Olney to an annual Race with the fastest time winning. Olney, of course, readily accepted the challenge, and the two Towns have competed each year ever since.

General Race Information

Date: Shrove Tuesday.
Starting Line: Pedestrian Crossing, Market Place, Olney.
Time: 11.55 a.m.
Course: From Market Place to the Parish Church of St. Peter and St. Paul.
Distance: 415 yards.
Many great prizes, all of which are kindly donated by local businesses. There is a prize for each runner.

How Olney Celebrates

Pancake Day in Olney is a hive of activity and there is plenty going on apart from the race. A Shriving Service is held in the Parish Church and some of the Olney Hymns are sung in remembrance of William Cowper and the Rev. John Newton and, leaders of the local churches preach a homily in turn. The Church is always full for this traditional and prestigious service and there is standing room only for those who do not arrive in good time. There are many more activities in the Town to enjoy as well as a number of establishments serving a variety of good old-fashioned pancakes.

A Typical Programme of Events

10.00 am   Pancakes and light refreshments are served in several places
             throughout the Town.
10.30 am   The Children's race.
11.55 am   The main Race.
12.15 pm   The Shriving Service at St. Peter and St. Paul's Church.
6.30 pm   The Transatlantic call comes through.
7.30 pm   Cheese and Wine Evening held in the Church Hall. The prizes are
             given out and entertainment is laid on, (ticket-only event).

Do you fancy having a go?

It's great fun and makes for a very memorable day!

Conditions of Entry and the Rules....

1. You must have lived in the Town for at least three months prior to the Race.
2. Minimum age is 18; there is no maximum age.
3. Traditional costume must be worn - headscarf and apron.
4. A traditional pancake must be tossed; once at the start and once during the Race.

Tradition and Custom.

21

5. You must keep hold of your pan and pancake until you reach the end

6. You will be required to attend the Shriving Service afterwards and any other events as requested by the Pancake Committee

7. Expect a kiss from either the Vicar or Bell-ringer – or both if you win

8. If you are lucky and win more than three times, you must stand down and give the others a chance

9. All winners' names and times are recorded in Church records

10. The event is subject to publicity; be prepared to have your photograph taken

Pancake Facts

The World's Largest Pancake

The world's largest pancake was made by the Co-operative Union Ltd in Rochdale, Lancashire on the 13th August 1994, to celebrate 150 years of the company's trading. It measured 49ft, 3" in diameter, was 1" deep and weighed 3 tonnes.

Important Ingredients

Flour	for	The staff of life
Milk	for	Innocence and purity
Salt	for	Incorruptibility
Eggs	for	Creativity

Superstitions

The French have a number of superstitions about pancakes. In Provence, for instance, there is a belief that if you hold a coin in your left hand whilst making or running with a pancake, you will become rich. And in Brie, it is an ancient tradition to give the first pancake of a batch made to the hen that laid the eggs –which makes a lot of sense and is not a bad idea, because the first pancake is often the worst one!

Napoleon and Josephine were reputed to have been pancake fanatics and they believed that dropping a pancake brought bad luck, in fact Napoleon blamed the failure of his Russian campaign on a pancake he had dropped some years earlier at Malmaison. This superstition is not only held by the French – it has also been passed down through generations in England.

And The Winners Are.....
Bold print denotes the winner

1948	Olney	Nellie Bosworth		1962	**Olney**	**Carole Vorley**
					Liberal	Vickie campbell
1949	Olney	Kathleen Powers		1963	Olney	Linda Risby
					Liberal	**Mary Barrington**
1950	**Olney**	**Florence Callow**		1964	**Olney**	**Bridget Lowrie**
	Liberal	Billie Warden			Liberal	Grace Kostreva
1951	**Olney**	**Isobel Dix**		1965	Olney	Jennifer Andrews
	Liberal	Emmagene "Genie" Bruce			**Liberal**	**Grace Riggs**
1952	Olney	Isobel Dix		1966	Olney	Janet Bunker
	Liberal	**Joan Zimmerman**			**Liberal**	**Rachel Crites**
1953	**Olney**	**Isobel Dix**		1967	**Olney**	**Janet Bunker**
	Liberal	Binnie Dick			Liberal	Lynda Fox
1954	Olney	Joan Keech		1968	**Olney**	**Mary Dix**
	Liberal	**Binnie Dick**			Liberal	Janice Grant
1955	Olney	Doris Millward		1969	**Olney**	**Sylvia Winstanley**
	Liberal	**Binnie Dick**			Liberal	Raneta Pomery
1956	Olney	Cicely Sparrow		1970	Olney	Sylvia Winstanley
	Liberal	**Nina Jordan**			**Liberal**	**Kathleen West**
1957	**Olney**	**Sandra Sibley**		1971	Olney	Ruth Faulkner
	Liberal	Mary Collingwood			**Liberal**	**Barbara Rinehart**
1958	**Olney**	**Sandra Sibley**		1972	Olney	Ella Crouch
	Liberal	Mary Collingwood			**Liberal**	**Kathleen West**
1959	Olney	Bridget Lowrie		1973	Olney	Ella Crouch
	Liberal	**Mary Collingwood**			**Liberal**	**Pat Clark**
1960	**Olney**	**Carole Vorley**		1974	Olney	Sallyann Faulkner
	Liberal	Anne E. Hunter			**Liberal**	**Patricia Cheeks**
1961	Olney	Carole Vorley		1975	Olney	Sallyann Faulkner
	Liberal	**Carolyn McGlamery**			**Liberal**	**Shelia Turner**

1976	Olney	Susan Hillier
	Liberal	**Shelia Turner**
1977	Olney	Sallyann Faulkner
	Liberal	**Mary Bender**
1978	Olney	June staham
	Liberal	**Stephanie Wagner**
1979	**Olney**	**Julie Perks**
	Liberal	Barbara McWilliams
1980	Olney	No winner course blocked
	Liberal	Shelia Turner
1981	**Olney**	**Rosemary Ludgate**
	Liberal	Gillian Brewer
1982	Olney	Rosemary Ludgate
	Liberal	**Barbara McCafferey**
1983	**Olney**	**Linda Carey**
	Liberal	Joyce Heeb
1984	**Olney**	**Louise Fitzgerald**
	Liberal	Mona Canaday
1985	**Olney**	**Sally Swallow**
	Liberal	Marcia Streiff
1986	**Olney**	**Elizabeth Bartlett**
	Liberal	Shelly Welch
1987	**Olney**	**Elizabeth Bartlett**
	Liberal	Marcia Streiff
1988	**Olney**	**Lesley Byrne**
	Liberal	Marcia Streiff
1989	**Olney**	**Lesley Byrne**
	Liberal	Donetta Schindler
1990	Olney	Alison Steele
	Liberal	**Carla Patterson**
1991	**Olney**	**Alison steele**
	Liberal	Donetta Schindler
1992	Olney	Susan Jones
	Liberal	**Vicky Van Sickle**
1993	Olney	Lesley Byrne
	Liberal	**Mindy Amerin**
1994	**Olney**	**Clare whittle**
	Liberal	Lisa Biddle
1995	**Olney**	**Jackie Bowden**
	Liberal	Lou Anne Baker

Winner 2003, Juliet Minter.

1996	Olney	Dawn Gallyot
	Liberal	**Christina Wilbers**
1997	Olney	Avril Sowman
	Liberal	**Christina Wilbers**
1998	**Olney**	**Natalie Thomas**
	Liberal	Christy Riffel
1999	Olney	Natalie Thomas
	Liberal	**Lisa Spellman**
2000	Olney	Avril Sowman
	Liberal	**Lisa Spellman**
2001	Olney	Juliet Minter
	Liberal	**Lisa Spellman**
2002	Olney	Juliet Minter
	Liberal	**Melissa Hurler**
2003	Olney	Juliet Minter
	Liberal	**Sherry Beavis**
2004	Olney	Andrea Rawlings
	Liberal	**Sherry Beavis**

From the inside looking out

(Or should I say from the rear looking forward)
By Chris Carter

On the Wednesday before the race a certain person by the name of Tony Evans came into the Orchard Press office in Stanley Court where I once worked and duly presented me with a headscarf! What can a girl do when she is put under so much pressure? I succumbed to the challenge.

Now six days is hardly enough time to prepare for a 415-yard dash when you can't remember the last time that you ran for a bus but in for a penny in for a pound. So on the Tuesday, carrying my pan and pancake and duly clad in the said headscarf, apron, skirt, socks and trainers (fashion gurus world-wide must have been having kittens), I arrived on the Market Place around 11.15 am and mustered with the other entrants. It seemed as if the world press was present and I hadn't had my picture taken so often since my wedding day in 1978.

Then we gathered outside the Olney Delicatessen by the plaque on the wall which denotes the start of the race for a false start so the press could get their pictures. Then back to the start for the real thing. At 11.55 am we were told to toss our pancakes and then the moment of truth - ready, steady, go – and we were off!

I wasn't doing too badly until I got level with Teapots when my pancake took on a life of its own and jumped out of the pan - so I had to stop and pick it up. It looked wonderful seasoned with tarmac!! It was about then that 74- year old Muriel Simpson decided she couldn't wait for me any longer and sped of into the distance. Well never mind, she's only 24 years older than me!! By this time I was beginning to run out of breath (smoking seriously damages your chances of winning the Pancake Race) but I made it round the corner and shouted to the crowd " Where's the end?"

The crowd were brilliant, they could see that I was struggling and they cheered me on to the end, where more photographs were taken after I had been presented with a card proudly letting the world know that I had come a very predictable **LAST**. After a short break, the runners and myself were led to the Cowley Room in the Church Tower where a very welcome drink was waiting for us, together with our coats and bags. We then had a chance to get our breath back before the Shriving Service began. From the viewpoint in the choir stalls I could see that the church was full to capacity and during the service we sang the Olney Hymns, prayers were said and Juliet Minter was presented with her prize for winning. Then it was back to work for the afternoon, although I can't say that there was an awful lot done by me that afternoon, I was on too much of a high.

Then home for tea and a quick look at "Look East" on the BBC. Yes, there I was, full frame practically crawling up to the church and gasping for breath.

The day didn't stop there though, it continued into the evening with a Cheese and Wine party in the Church Hall. Upon arrival we were presented with a voucher for a free glass of wine and the buffet (which was a lot more than just cheese and wine) was served. Whilst we were eating we were treated to some wonderful Irish music from the Grafton Street Band, featuring John Homans of Francis Jackson Homes on the drums. Some of us even had enough energy to have a bit of a dance.

Once we had eaten it was time for the presentation of the prizes and everyone was given a "goody bag". I won't tell you what was in it as it will only spoil the surprise for future runners. I was then presented with a special prize for coming **LAST**. At the end of the evening I saw Tony Evans and thanked him for cajoling me into taking part - it was one of the most enjoyable days of my life.

So come on girls, we don't all have to be elite runners to join in the fun and take part in a very historical (or should I say hysterical) event. Sign up for it; you'll be really glad that you did, even if you do ache for a couple days. In this troubled world we need to keep these traditions alive, and thriving.

Floral Fiesta

The Floral Fiesta in Olney is the annual summertime event that is normally held over a week in June / July. The activities and events are organised by the Olney Floral Fiesta Committee and are well spread out over the week with the Grand Parade through the Town heralding the finale on the Saturday.

The Olney Floral Fiesta Committee, which consists of about 10 members, has numerous helpers and associates which are known as the Friends. However, the Committee is always on the lookout for more willing helpers, so if you fancy an opportunity to contribute especially if you are new to the area, it's a great way of getting to know the Town and to make new friends. Anyone interested should contact one of the members of the Committee for further information.

As for the younger girls of the Town, there is also the excitement of electing a Floral Fiesta Queen and Princesses every year. The Queen and her escorts are required to attend various public events held in the Town, as well as holding court on occasions. So if you have ever dreamed of being a Queen or a Princess, here's

Clowning around.

The Royal Carriage.

your chance. It is a responsibility, of course, but it is a thrilling experience one that's full of fun.

The aim of the Fiesta week is to raise some much-needed funds for the many clubs, groups and organisations that exist in the immediate locality. So by enjoying yourselves you are also contributing towards some well-deserving causes in the Town.

The following are some of the typical events that take place during Fiesta week although, of course, these are liable to change -

The Cherry Fair	A Treasure Hunt	The Duck Race
The Raft Race	Queen's Crowning	Church Services
Teddy Bears' Picnic	Fiesta Quiz	Fiesta Bingo
Band Night	Grand Parade	Festival
Men's Pancake Race	Parade	Day Arena Events

The Cherry Fair

The Cherry Fair is one of the first events of the Fiesta week and is held on or near the 29th June, the Feast Day of St Peter and St Paul, the patron saints of the Parish Church. The fair is an ancient custom in Olney, designed to celebrate the end of the cherry harvest and there was much drinking and making merry going on in Olney.

The Fair is usually held in Glebe field, opposite the Old Vicarage, and is host to numerous local stalls, which typically includes a tombola, raffles and the infamous tug of war competition. This competition is between the pupils of Olney first school and the adult members of the Olney Rugby Club. No guessing who wins hands down every year!! It is a highly entertaining spectacle and well worth watching. The refreshment stall provides that much-needed cup of tea and there are some delicious homemade cakes available, which makes it a very popular gathering point.

The Cherry Fair is hosted and organised by the Parish Church and the funds raised help to support the necessary but expensive upkeep of one of the Town's most precious assets.

The Duck Race

Pretty as a picture

A bygone court from my school days.

The Duck Race, together with the Raft Race, is usually held one weekend afternoon during Fiesta week. The event comes under the wing of the Young Women's Members Group of Olney Youth Club and the money raised from the Race contributes towards some of their adventurous activities.

The race starts with the launching of little rubber ducks from the weir bridge and the winner is the first duck to reach the main bridge. It all sounds very simple and straightforward but if the wind is blowing in the wrong direction, there's no telling where the ducks may end up and the journey is often hilarious.

The Duck Race is a simple bit of fun that's enjoyed by children of all ages and there is no difficulty in purchasing tickets either, before, or on the day.

The Raft Race

The Raft Race normally starts after the Duck Race with homemade rafts launched into the water just near the weir in Emberton Park.

Aim of the race:

For contestants to row their rafts as fast as possible to the finishing line at the river's steps in the Recreation Ground just off East Street. Having a themed raft, with the contestants dressing up accordingly, is actively encouraged, and prizes are awarded in the following categories -

Men's Commercial	Ladies' Commercial	Most Entertaining Raft
Men's Private	Ladies' Private	
Men - 17 years and under	Ladies - 17 years and under	

Typical Questions asked:

How long is the course?

Roughly, about 1.5 miles.

How long does it take to complete?

This totally depends on the individuals and their rafts but anything from around 20 minutes, for those on a mission, to 2 hours for the less ambitious.

Can you see the rafts as they complete the course?

Yes, from the Mill onwards but it is a fair distance to walk and one that is not best suited to wheelchairs, buggies, the elderly or infirm. Although the crossings through the meadow have recently being upgraded by the Fishing Club, it is still difficult for wheelchairs and buggies, which need to be lifted over at certain points. And it needs to be remembered that the weather can be very hot at this time of the year.

For those that do want to walk the course, head for the hills as they say – the Clifton Hills area - via the cemetery and to the right until you reach the river, which you follow to the recreation ground and the finishing line.

One thing to consider before you go walking off. You will pass through privately owned fields in which animals frequently graze, so please ensure the gates are closed after you, and do not leave litter en-route. Furthermore, if you suffer from asthma or hay fever, be aware that the pollen count in this area can be very high at this time of year.

Rules and Regulations

1. All rafts must be hand made - small ready-made boats and canoes are not permitted.
2. Rafts must be sturdy and capable of taking part.
3. Life jackets / buoyancy aids must be worn at all times.
4. It is strictly forbidden to interfere with any other rafts along the course.
5. Any contestant deemed unfit to participate due to excess alcohol will not be allowed to enter the race.

The Grand Parade

Fiesta week reaches a climax with the Grand Parade along the High Street on the final Saturday and it's one of those rare occasions when the traffic into the Town is stopped throughout the procession. Each year's Parade has a chosen theme, with several floats, including a decorated carriage for the Fiesta Queen and her Princesses. Bands, dancing groups and costume-clad walkers also participate as well as buses, trailers and prams – in fact anything on wheels – is actively encouraged. The more the merrier, as they say...

The procession sets off at 1pm from the recreation ground, turning right into East Street and heading towards the High Street via Holes Lane. The Parade then travels southwards down the High Street, clockwise around the Market Place and back northwards on the same route, finishing back in the recreation ground.

During the Parade, easily identified volunteers walk amongst the crowd rattling collecting pots in aid of Fiesta funds. The generosity of the public on these occasions has enabled the Olney Floral Fiesta Committee to improve the Parade and the festivities each year to the present high standard. But it is well recognised there is always scope for further improvement and may the bountiful onlookers continue to drop their spare cash into the multicoloured collection buckets as they pass.

Judging

Tiger Moths leading the way 2003.

The floats are judged on the basis of entries for adults and children and prizes awarded accordingly. Similarly, Fancy Dress is judged and rewarded in the following categories:- under 8 years, 8 – 16 years, adults and walking groups.

Olney's Floral Fiesta 2003.

Following the Parade, the supporting festivities begin and continue through to the early evening.

The Men's Pancake Race

It's quirky, it's different, and yes, we know it's the wrong time of year for a pancake race, but this has become a popular event and takes place during the main Parade.

The Race begins shortly after 1pm and just before the Parade reaches the High Street.

The starting line is conveniently and aptly outside the Two Brewers Pub and the finishing line is at the pedestrian crossing on the Market Place, where, of course, the ladies' race starts on Pancake Day.

It is a really easy course to run (especially after some reinforcement in the Two Brewers beforehand). Just one simple, straight mad-dash on the level to the end. So come on lads have a go! Although you will be required to wear the traditional gear – apron and headscarf and the weather should be good to you at that time of year, which means that there will be no icicles or biting wind blowing up and around your hairy bits. It's just a harmless bit of fun, with some good prizes for the winners and runners-up – and of course there is always the Bull by the finishing line!!

Other things to see and do on Parade Day

In the main Fiesta arena to the rear of the Recreation Ground in East Street, the following are typical attractions for the day -

Martial Arts Display	Wildcat CheerLeaders Flypast
Raffles	Olney First School Dance Experience
Floral Prize Giving	Tug-of-War
Motorama's Prize-winners Parade	

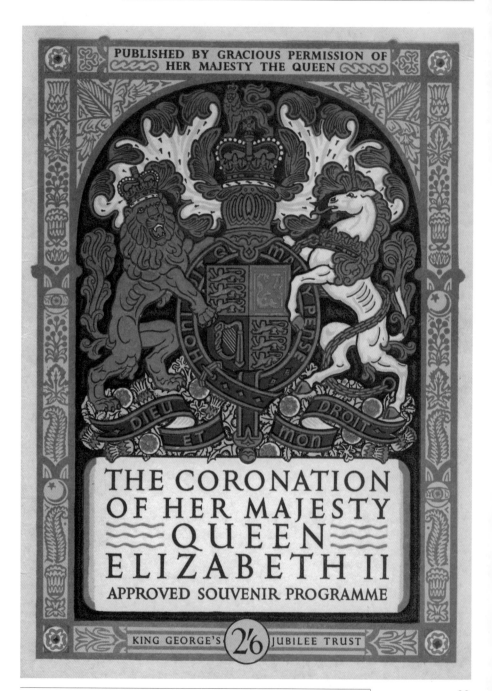

Remembrance Day

At the 11th hour on the 11th day of the 11th month each year, the nation, including Olney, is united in a two-minute silence to remember those who lost their lives while serving, protecting and defending our country during the two World Wars and other conflicts. Millions of servicemen and women lost their lives in battle and many thousands are buried in and around the trenches where they fell. In Olney these brave people, especially our local inhabitants, are remembered and honoured not only in services around the Town on Remembrance Day but also in other ways.

The War Memorial: Olney Market Place

"To the glory of god
And in the memory of the men
From this town
Who fell in the Great War 1914 –1919
Their name liveth for evermore".

Fact File

Date Built: 1921
By who: J.G. Pullen & Sons
Cost: £649.12
Unveiled: 1921 by General Lord Horne
The Monument: A monolithic form with a square tapering pillar base and moulded plinth, mounted upon three steps, which are all Derbyshire stone.

Olney's Book of Remembrance

Olney's Book of Remembrance is dedicated to the service men and women from Olney who died for their country during Word War 1 and World War 2. One of the soldiers, Alec Morgan, who is mentioned in more detail in one of the following chapters, spent many years assembling a personal account of fellow soldiers who served with him during the 2nd World War. Overtime Alec managed to build up a comprehensive record of each serviceman who came from Olney. His work was deemed

War Memorial Olney c.1921.

an extremely important document for Olney and was encapsulated into the Book of Remembrance, which is now on display in the north aisle of the Parish Church.

Roll of Honour

The Roll of Honour lists were produced by the following people, who have very kindly given permission for this material to be included in this publication.

World War 1:   Martin Edwards
World War 2:   Mrs Mona Morgan, wife of the late Alec Morgan

OLNEY'S ROLL OF HONOUR.

Harry Andrews	William Hopper
Arthur William Baguley	Walter Huckle
Frank Barnes	Alfred Charles Johnson
Thomas Barnes	Charles Johnson
John Berrill	Arthur Jones
Arthur Campion	Arthur G. Percy Joyce
Philip Chapman	William Kitchener
William Chater	Ernest Limbrey
Hugh Church	Joseph Longland
Sidney Church	Frank Lyman
Albert Clare	Alfred Millward
Harry Coles	John Millward
Herbert Coles	Melbourn Muskett
Bert Coles	Frederick Newbury
Arthur James Cooper	Ernest Parrott
Sidney Charles Davis	Walter Partridge
Edward Edmunds	Vincent Pater
Leslie Morier Evans	Charles Perkins
Thomas Fairey	Horace Perkins
Alfred John Fiel	Percy Rice
Frederick Freeman	George Richardson
Harry William Freeman	Alfred Robinson
Horace Freeman	Alfred Underwood
Albert Henry Gathergood	Benjamin Wallinger
Randolph Goldsmith	John Walton
Cyril Grey	Bert Ward
Edwin Harris	William Whiting
Stanley Haseldine	Charles Wilford
Ernest Hinde	George Willey
Charles Stanley Hipwell	John Wilson
Harry Reginald Hipwell	Albert Wm. Wrighting

✝

The Order of Service

AT THE

Unveiling

OF THE

War Memorial

AT

Olney, Bucks.,

ON

Sunday, May 1st, 1921,

at 4 p.m.,

BY

General Lord Horne, of Stirkoke,
G.C.B., K.C.M.G.

F. STANLEY, PRINTER, OLNEY.

35

WW1 Roll of Honour

Andrews, Victor, Ernest, The Leys, Olney. Army 152818, Royal Artillery. Missing in action.

Andrews, Harry Prov. Lance Corporal 4414, 3rd Dragoon Guards (Prince of Wales' Own). Killed in action 1st June 1915 in France. Born and resident of Olney, enlisted at Bedford.

Baculey, Arthur William Sapper 522415, 486 Field Company, Royal Engineers. Died Sunday 24th November 1918. Aged 25. Son of Arthur and Elizabeth Baguley of No 11 Wellingborough Road, Olney. Buried in Alexandria (HADRA) War Memorial Cemetery, Egypt, Grave E 22.

Barnes, Frank Private 10155, 1st Battalion, Bedfordshire Regiment. Killed in action 16th March 1915 in France. Born and resident of Olney, enlisted at Bedford.

Barnes, Thomas William Private 4236 1st Battalion, Northamptonshire Regiment. Killed in action 3rd November 1917 in France. Born in Olney, enlisted at Northampton.

Berrill, John Private 18311, 11th Battalion, Royal Warwickshire Regiment. Died of wounds 11th August 1916 in France. Born at Clifton Reynes, resident of Olney, enlisted at Bletchley. Formerly 22949, Somerset Light Infantry.

Campion, Arthur Private 33780, 8th Battalion, Princess Charlotte of Wales' Royal Berkshire Regiment. Killed in action 16th November 1917 in France. Born and resident of Olney, enlisted at Bletchley. Formerly 28567, Oxfordshire & Buckinghamshire Light Infantry.

Campion, Phillip. No information available.

Chapman, Phillip Private 50653, 1st Battalion, Cheshire Regiment. Killed in action on Monday 17th June 1918 in France, age 31. Born Ecton, Northamptonshire, enlisted at Bedford. Son of Mr C Chapman of Park Farm, Olney and the late Mrs Chapman. Formerly 20655, Bedfordshire Regiment.

Chater, William Private 20403, 8th Battalion, Bedfordshire Regiment. Killed in action 25th September 1916 in France. Born and resident of Olney, enlisted at Bedford.

Church, Hugh Lance Corporal 306561, 1st / 8th Territorial Battalion. Killed in action 25th September 1916 in France. Born and resident of Olney, enlisted at Bedford.

Church, Sidney Charles Private 18469, 1st Battalion, Warwickshire Regiment. Killed in action 29th March 1918 in France. Born Warrington, enlisted at Bletchley, resident of Olney. Formerly 24310, Somerset Light Infantry.

Clare, Albert Private 3 / 11153, 1st Battalion, Northamptonshire Regiment. Killed in action 9th May 1915 in France. Born in Olney, enlisted at Northampton.

Coles, Bertie Private CH / 18886 (s), 1st Royal Marine Battalion, Royal Naval Division, Royal Marine Light Infantry. Died Friday 26th October 1917, aged 25. Son of Esther Coles, 14 Near Town, Olney.

Coles, Harry. No information available.

Coles, Herbert. No information available.

Cooper, Arthur James Private 2000240, 1st / 4th Battalion, Northamptonshire Regiment. Died of wounds 2nd December 1917 in Palestine. Born Olney, enlisted at Rushden, Northants.

Davis, Sidney Charles Private 19972, 8th Battalion Princess Charlotte of Wales' Royal Berkshire Regiment. Killed in action 3rd September 1916 in France. Born in Olney, enlisted at Oxford, resident of Kingston Blount, Oxon.

Edmunds, John Edward Private 11480, Coldstream Guards. Killed in action 22nd December 1914 in France. Born and resident of Olney, enlisted at Exeter.

Evans, Leslie Morier Second Lieutenant, Royal Army Corps. Killed in action 12th November 1917.

Fairey, Thomas Walter Private 2672211, 5th Battalion Oxfordshire & Buckinghamshire Light Infantry. Killed in action 23rd March 1918 in France. Born and resident of Olney, enlisted at Bletchley.

Field, Alfred John Private 26231, 2nd Battalion, Oxfordshire & Buckinghamshire Light Infantry. Died of wounds, 30th April 1917 in France. Born and resident of Olney, enlisted at Bletchley.

Freeman, Frederick Corporal 9286, 1st Battalion, Northamptonshire Regiment. Killed in action 17th September 1914 in France. Born in Olney, enlisted at Northampton.

Freeman, Harry William Private 22976, 5th Battalion, Oxfordshire & Buckinghamshire Light Infantry. Killed in action 3rd May 1917 in France. Born and resident of Olney, enlisted at Bletchley.

Freeman, Horace Private 202672, 2nd / 4th Battalion, Oxfordshire & Buckinghamshire Light Infantry. Killed in action 21st March 1918 in France. Born and resident of Olney, enlisted at Bletchely.

Gathergood, Albert Henry   Listed as Henry on the War Memorial. Private 27961, 8th Battalion East Yorkshire. Died of wounds 31st March 1917 in France. Enlisted at Rushden.

Goldsmith, Randolph Frank Private Ch 2153(s). Div., Royal Marine Light Infantry. Died 8th September 1917 in France age 30. Son of Samuel Goldsmith of Olney; husband of May Goldsmith of 47 Midland Road, Olney. Buried in Bailleul Road, East Cemetery, St Laurent- Blangy, Pas de Calais France, Grave 1. Q1.

Grey, Cyril. No information available.

Harris, Edwin. Private 27349, 6th Battalion, Bedfordshire Regiment. Killed in action 8th October 1917 in France. Born in Olney, enlisted at Ampthill, Beds. Resident of Bozeat, Northants.

Haseldine, Stanley Private 36395, 1st Battalion, Royal Warwickshire Regiment. Died 30th August 1918 in France. Born and resident of Olney, enlisted at Aylesbury.

Hinde, Ernest Private 48610, 5th Battalion, Princess Charlotte of Wales' Royal Berkshire Regiment. Killed in action 29th April 1918 in France. Born in Olney, enlisted at Bletchley, resident of Lavendon. Formerly 40447, Somerset Light Infantry.

Hipwell, Charles Stanley Lieutenant, Queens' Westminster Rifles. Killed in action 15th October 1916 in France. Second

37

son of John Charles Hipwell and Annie Eva Hipwell. Born 23rd September 1887. Buried in Marceuil Cemetery, France. In September 23rd 1916 he led a successful raid into the enemy trenches, which resulted in the capture of prisoners. He engaged a fire bay full of Germans and silenced them with his revolver, remaining on the parapet whilst his men crossed the hostile wire and thereafter the last man had left for our lines. He went out again under continuous fire to search " no mans land" for a wounded man. The success of this raid was due to the determination and resourceful leading for which he was awarded the Military Cross.

Hipwell, Harry Reginald Second Lieutenant, 4th Ross Highland Battalion, Seaforth Highlanders & Machine Gun Corps. Killed in action Monday 23rd April 1917 in France. Buried in Brown's Copse Cemetery, Roeux, Pas de Calais. Grave VII. A. 30.

Hooper, George William Private 3811, 1st / 4th Battalion, Northamptonshire Regiment. Died of wounds at sea 3rd August 1915. Born in Olney, enlisted at Northampton.

Huckle, Walter Private 267195, 1st / 2nd Battalion, Oxfordshire & Buckinghamshire Light Infantry. Died Saturday 31st March 1917 in France age 35. Born in Olney, enlisted at Bletchley. Resident of Clifton Reynes, son of Elizabeth Huckle. Buried in Tertry Communal Cemetery, Somme, France. Grave B.1.

Johnson, Alfred Charles Private 201277, 4th Battalion Essex Regiment. Killed in action 26th March 1917 in France. Born in Olney, enlisted at Kettering, resident of Bozeat, Northants.

Johnson, Charles Private 19712, 9th Service Battalion, Gloucestershire. Died of wounds Saturday 9th October 1915 in France. Born in Buckingham, enlisted at Oxford. Son of Mr W. Johnston, 81 High Street, Olney. Buried in St Pierre Cemetery, Amiens, Somme, France. Grave.1.A.10.

Jones, Arthur Private 9415, 5th Battalion Northamptonshire Regiment. Killed in action 15th July 1917 in France. Born in Olney, enlisted in Northampton.

Joyce, Arthur George Percy Private 41264, 8th Battalion Bedfordshire Regiment. Killed in action on 3rd December 1917 in France. Born in Olney, enlisted at Northampton. Resident of Rushden, Northants. Formerly 38540 of the Northampton Regiment.

Joyce, Peter. No information available.

Kitchener, William Private 12125, 4th Battalion, South of Wales Borderers. Died of wounds 31st January 1917 in Mesopotamia. Born in Olney, enlisted at Northampton.

Limbery, Albert Ernest Private 30678, 17th Lancers, Duke of Cambridge's Own. Killed in action 8th August 1918 in France. Born and resident of Olney, enlisted at Bedford.

Longland, Joseph Private 2672208, 2nd / 1st Buckinghamshire Battalion, and Oxfordshire and Buckinghamshire Light Infantry. Killed in action 2nd April 1917 in France. Born and resident of Olney, enlisted at Bletchley.

Lyman, Frank Rifleman 8129, 3rd Battalion, Rifle Brigade, The Prince Consort's Own. Killed in action 23rd October 1914 in France. Born and resident of Olney, enlisted at Bletchley.

Millward, Arthur Charles Private 20339, **8th Battalion, Bedfordshire Regiment.** Killed in action 15th September 1916 in France. Born Northampton, enlisted at Bedford, resident of Olney.

Millward, John Percy Private 5802, **1st / 4th Battalion, Oxfordshire & Buckinghamshire Light Infantry.** Died of wounds 1st September 1916 in France. Born and resident of Olney, enlisted at Bletchley.

Mobbs, Edgar Roberts Lieutenant Colonel, **7th Battalion Northamptonshire Regiment.** Killed in action at the battle of Passchendale on Tuesday, 31st July 1917 whilst charging at an enemy machine gun post. Age 37. Son of Oliver and Elizabeth Mobbs, Northampton.

Muskett, Melbourne Private 23581, **4th Battalion Bedfordshire Regiment.** Killed in action 13th November 1916. Born and resident of Olney, enlisted at Ampthill.

Newbury, Frederick Private 29066, **Royal Army Medical Corps.** Died 6th November 1915 at Gallipoli. Born and resident of Olney, enlisted at Northampton.

Parrot, Ernest. No information available.

Partridge, Walter Private 9095, **2nd Battalion Northamptonshire Regiment.** Killed in action 9th May 1915 in France. Born in Olney, enlisted in Northampton.

Pater, George Vincent Private 51287, **10th Battalion, Worcestershire Regiment.** Killed in action 18th June 1918 in France. Born and resident of Olney, enlisted at Bletchley.

Perkins, Charles Private 33655, **2nd Battalion, Bedfordshire Regiment.** Killed in action 25th June 1918 in France. Born and resident of Olney, enlisted at Bedford. Formerly 2004, Bedfordshire Yeomanry.

Perkins, Horace Thomas Private 18448, **11th Battalion, Royal Warwickshire Regiment.** Killed in action 10th April 1917 in France. Born and resident of Olney, enlisted at Bletchley. Formerly 24031, Somerset Light Infantry.

Rice, Percy Ernest Driver 272908, **81st Battery. Royal Field Artillery.** Died at home on Monday 9th September 1918 aged 27. Born Northampton, enlisted at Oxford

Richardson, George Corporal 200151, **5th Battalion, Bedfordshire Regiment.** Killed in action 2nd November 1917 in Palestine. Born and resident of Olney, enlisted at Northampton.

Robinson, Alfred Private 29057, **Royal Army Medical Corps.** Died 28th June 1916 in Mesopotamia. Born and resident of Olney, enlisted at Northampton.

Underwood, Alfred Private 60101, **26th Battalion, Royal Fusiliers, City of London Regiment.** Killed in action 20th September 1917 in France. Formerly 46386, 3rd Battalion, Bedfordshire Regiment.

Wallinger, Benjamin Private 3/11131, **2nd Battalion, Northamptonshire Regiment.** Killed in action 31st July 1917 in France. Born Buckingham, enlisted at Rushden, Northants.

Walton, John Private 28240, **1st Battalion, Prince Albert's Somerset Light Infantry.** Killed in action 4th October 1917 in France. Born Northampton, enlisted at Bletchley, resident of Olney.

Ward, Bert Private 20426, 8th Battalion, Bedfordshire Regiment. Killed in action 20th April 1916 in France. Born and resident of Olney, enlisted at Bedford.

Whiting, William Henry Acting Corporal 11129, 8th Battalion, Lincolnshire Regiment. Killed in action 3rd July 1916 in France. Born and resident of Olney, enlisted at Grimsby.

Wilford, Charles. No information available.

Willey, George Private 26203, 5th Battalion, Oxfordshire and Buckinghamshire Light Infantry. Killed in action 28th February 1917 in France. Born and resident of Olney, enlisted Bletchley.

Wilson, John. No information available.

Wrighting, Albert William Private 200157, 5th Battalion, Bedfordshire Regiment. Died 14th November 1918 in Palestine. Born, enlisted and resident of Olney.

WW2 Roll of Honour

Barcock, Arthur Yardley Road, Olney. Army. 7630961. Reported killed in action, 7th October 1940, age 24.

Barrick, Jack Panter Resident of Olney. Royal Navy, missing in action.

Bosworth, Frederick Near Town, Olney. Army 1626336. Killed in action aged 33, buried in Olney.

Brent, Herbert James Newton Street, Olney. Army 5952312. Killed in action.

Brimley, Richard George Moores Hill, Olney. Royal Navy. Killed in action 1940.

Cowley, Samuel Henry Clifton House, High Street, Olney. Major of the Beds & Herts Regiment. Killed in action on 19th July 1944, aged 33, buried in France.

Haines, John Marriott Resident of Olney. Royal Air Force. Killed in action, buried in Olney.

Hanson, David James High Street, Olney. RNVR, Sub-lieutenant, died 31st May 1944, aged 22.

Holton, Jack Resident of Olney. Royal Air Force 1624091. Reported as missing in action.

Hooton, Peter Wellingborough Road, Olney. Army 1426891. Killed in action.

Mackenzie, Gilbert Resident of Newton Street, Olney. R.A.F 5183Y21. Sergeant Pilot, killed in ariel combat.

Petit, Charles Edward Resident of Moores Hill, Olney. R.A.F 754782. Killed on active service, 2nd October 1940, aged 24.

Philpot, John William Resident of Silver End. Olney. Army 5385280. Reported killed in action.

Ruffhead, Angus Walter Resident of Church Street, Olney. RAF Flight Lieutenant, killed in aerial combat.

Sibley, Leslie Reginald Resident of Cowper Street, Olney. R.A.F. 1200327. Killed in active service, 20th October 1943, buried in Olney.

Tidmarsh, George Frederick Resident of Weston Road, Olney. Army 7664401. Killed in a road accident.

Tompkins, Anthony Peter Warrick Terrace, Olney. Army 1403023. Killed in action, buried in Normandy, France.

Willey, Stanley East Street, Olney. Army 5953196. Reported missing, killed in action.

This letter was found whilst researching through old archives of the soldiers from the 2nd World War who came from Olney and it makes for an interesting read.

C O P Y.

...... Road,
KEMPSTON, Beds.

Dear Mr. Willey,

18 August, 46.

Your letter is not the first that has arrived asking for particulars cocerning the sinking of the HOPUKU MARU, the prison ship on which your brother and I were travelling.
Ever since I have been home the War Office and the Regt. have been writing asking forall sorts of informationand I had the very unpleasant task of going through the Battn. lists confirming at least 50 deaths.
Before I try to answer your questions please accept my sincere condolences in the loss of your Brother Stan who I can personally say was indeed a most pleasant and cheeful companion.
If my letter is the cause of contenting your mind as to the exact circumstances under which he died I shall at least feel that I have done something to show how eternally grateful I am for being spared to join my family once again, sufficient to say that I have now settled down and daily forgetting the awful past 3½ years.
I'll not bother you with all that happened prior to the sinking of the ship enough is to say that the conditions on board hardly bear mention but if you are round this way at any time and you are really interested it will be my pleasure to tell you.
Two days before the sinking 21st Sept 1944 I was moved from which there were four Bedfords (Cpl. Wilton, Cpl. Gaylor your brother and myself) down into the bottom hold amidships as I was suffering from beri-beri.
All the fellows were in good health (as standards went at the time) and spirits were of the best. Each day the Bedfords managed to come and see me in turn and had on the day of the sinking returned to their space about 15 minutes before the attack 10.30 am. Our position at the time was 1½ days sailing at 10 knots per hour from Manila sailing in a NW direction and the course lay through very close waters as the Japs were trying to avoid the Allied Navy. The attack which was carried out entireky by USA planes was over in ½ hour and our ship was singled out being the biggest and got two aerial torpedoes and 3 bombs all being direct hits. The ship sank well within 5 mins being completely blown in two.
I feel sure that your brothers death must have been instantaneous for that part of the ship was completely blown out of the water in addition all hatch ladders were destroyed and the men battened down and overcrowded bad very badly. I myself was in the water about 4 hours and contacted a Pte. Ford who managed to stay with me until the end of the war. Every effort was made after the sinking right up to the time of my reaching England to try and trace any possible survivors of the Battalion.
In Manila where we were taken after release I visited every reception centre and went through the complete rolls and was able to gain information about quite a few.
Once again let me say that I feel sure your Brother could not have suffered any agony or discomfort (apart from those prevailing on the ship) before meeting his death which as I repeat must have been instanttaneous.
Hoping this letter will ease your anxiety and help you to bear your loss with greater comfort of mind.   Yours truly,   A.N. BURGESS.
- -
Extract from Mr. L.A. WIlley's letter, ... 10/92.
Quote He was taken prisoner at the fall of Singapore, forced to work on the death railway and was being transported to Japan to work down the copper mines. The ship he was on was sunk by USA planes. He was one who did not survive. UNQUOTE.

This refers to 5953196. Pte. Stan. WILLEY, (East Street, Olney).
Pioneer Platoon, HQ Coy. 5th Bn. Bedfordshire &
Hertfordshire Regiment.

The Origin of the Poppy

The tradition of wearing a poppy began in the 1920s when an American, Moina Michael, began wearing a poppy to work out of respect for those who had died during earlier conflicts. Others soon followed suit and the tradition soon became popular, then and after the publication of the war poem " In Flanders Field " in **1918**, the poppy was designated as the national symbol for Remembrance Day.

Today, millions of poppies are sold in Britain at this time of remembrance and the proceeds are donated to the Royal British Legion.

In Flanders Field

During the First World War **(1914 -1918)**, a 43 year-old Scottish born, Canadian solider, John Macrae, noticed that a field where he was engaged in battle was totally barren during the fighting, yet 17 days later the same field had exploded into a carpet of bright red poppies.

It was on the battlefield and during a lull in the fighting that John Macrae managed to scribble the 13 line poem, " In Flanders Field " onto a piece of paper. Macrae had been a poet, author, teacher and doctor before he gave it all up to fight for the allies but on his return he sent a copy of his poem to Punch Magazine in London who duly printed it - and the rest, as they say, is history.

Sadly, John died of pneumonia in Boulogne, France, on the **28th January 1918**, but his memory still lives on in a war bunker in Menim, Flanders. Subsequent findings have since shown that this poppy explosion was possibly due to large quantities of lime in the soil, which had been enhanced by the heavy bombardment and the ravages of battle deposited in the field. However, despite a gradual dissolution of the lime deposit over the decades since, the poppies still continue to flourish in the area.

In Flanders Field
By John Mc Crae, 1915

In Flanders field the poppies blow
Between the crosses, row on row
That mark our place; and in the sky
The Larks, still bravely singing, fly
Scarce heard amid the guns below.

We are the Dead. Short days ago
We lived, felt dawn, saw sunset glow,
Loved and were loved, and now we lie,
In Flanders fields.

Take up our quarrel with the foe:
To you from failing hands we throw
The torch: be yours to hold it high.
If ye break faith with us who die
We shall not sleep, though poppies grow
In Flanders fields.

Bonfire Night

" Remember, remember the 5th of November, gun powder, treason and plot.
We see no reason why gunpowder treason should ever be forgot".

Bonfire Night is closely related to an ancient Celtic festival called Samhain, a New Year's celebration and bonfires played an important part in the festival as they were considered to ward off evil spirits.

By the 1600s, Guy Fawkes had appeared on the scene and tried, albeit unsuccessfully, to blow up the Houses of Parliament but he was arrested and tortured, and later executed with his co-conspirators. In 1606, with Guy Fawkes no longer a threat to King and Country, Parliament decided to make the 5th of November a day of public thanksgiving and ever since this country has celebrated with bonfires and fireworks.

Olney remembers and celebrates this anniversary with a grand display of fireworks in the " **Barn Field** ", on the outskirts of Town. The event is organised and hosted by the Olney Floral Fiesta Committee and is always well attended by the residents of the town. Local children are encouraged to make a guy for The Guy Fawkes competition and they can also enter their Jack o' lanterns, left over from Halloween, into a another contest and prizes are awarded to winners of both competitions. As well as the spectacular firework display, a Beer Tent is available for the adults and a small fun fair is provided for the children.

Dickens of a Christmas

Dickens of a Christmas is a traditional event that takes place in Olney every year on a Sunday early in December, marking the countdown to Christmas.

The day is organised by the Olney Town Council, with the help of the Floral Fiesta Committee, and there is a buzz around all day with many and varied attractions throughout the Town. Being held on a Sunday makes it the most popular day of the year in Olney and thousands of people pour in from near and far. It is probably the only day in the year that we have congestion on our wide High Street pavements.

"All Aboard", Dickens of a Christmas 2003.

An Early Start

The day starts early, around 8 am, with Santa Claus touring the Town on his sleigh.

Good old-fashioned entertainment.

After this tour he heads towards the Market Place, where he spends the rest of the day receiving his many little visitors. By 10 am the festivities are in full swing and visitors start arriving in hordes. If the weather is fine, which seems to be the case more often than not, participants can wander leisurely around the Town enjoying the decorations and attractions.

Festive Spirit

A good majority of the shops in the town are open and bursting with festive spirit and, in keeping with the occasion, many of the shopkeepers and residents will be dressed in Dickensian costume. The Market Place has a host of stalls where it is possible to find that little something extra for the Christmas stocking, as well as some seasonal delicacies such as turkey rolls, minced pies and mulled wine. The pubs, cafes and restaurants all do a roaring trade on this day, especially if it happens to be raining.

44

As well as the shops and stalls, there are also street entertainers and horse-drawn carriages. The Cowper and Newton Museum and the Parish Church are also open during the day with exhibitions and refreshments laid on for the visitors.

A Break from the Cold

If weather conditions are bad and shelter is needed, retreats can be found in the Olney Centre, the Working Men's Club and the Church Hall which are - all in the High Street - and where more displays, exhibitions and stalls are in place. These are ideal places for a warm up - and a comfort station - and by paying a nominal entrance fee at any one, free admission will be granted to the other two.

Park and Ride

It can be almost impossible to drive into Olney on Dickens Day and with insufficient parking for such an influx, a Park and Ride service is laid on at both the northerly and southerly approaches to the Town. Just follow the signs and you will be able to leave your car, hop on the courtesy bus and in a matter of minutes you will be in the centre of the festivities.

Dickens Day in Olney is a wonderful occasion and a brilliant opportunity to initiate the Spirit of Christmas. There is something for everyone and each year, with the ever-growing support of an increasing number of visitors, it just gets better and better. Whilst admitting to being biased, we are confident you will find no better Christmas Fayre in Buckinghamshire than Olney's Dickens of a Christmas Day.

Based on B. Proud's Illustrations.

Folk Lore

Olney Folk Lore

Folk lore and devil lore often went hand-in-hand in days of yore, and this seems to have been the case in Olney. All of the following folk stories are centuries old and have been passed down through the ages by some of the Town's inhabitants, past and present. The following accounts have been re-adapted by the author to conform to modern language and terminology.

The Whirly Pits, Wellingborough Road

At the stroke of midnight one cold and dark night many, many years ago, the Prince of Darkness was reputed to have come thundering down the Warrington Road towards Olney. The reason for his mission was unknown but he travelled at great speed in a carriage that was steered by a headless horseman and pulled by four headless horses.

With ferocious speed and power the carriage plunged into the Whirly Pits and continued its journey via the legendary underground passage to Goosey Bridge, Weston Road. Here the carriage burst through the ground like a volcanic eruption, causing untold damage and destruction to the field where it stopped. It is said that, even today, any person standing astride this spot will feel the ground sway and shudder as if it's recalling the events of that fateful night.

The Devil in Olney

The Devil or Johann Faustus has been seen on numerous occasions in and around the Town and what follows are a few accounts of his visits.

So who was Johann Faustus?

Johann Faustus was some times locally known as the Devil in certain folk lore legends. And, it is also thought to have been derived from a Johann Faust, a German 16th century magician and philosopher and hero of several poetic and dramatic works, who was reputed to have sold his soul to the devil in exchange for power and knowledge.

The Nosey Neighbour

Whilst residing at a property (which no longer exists) at the northerly end of the Town, the Devil had become greatly annoyed by a female neighbour. The lady in question was, by all accounts, a nosey parker who had the most infuriating habit of watching him at every possible opportunity. There were numerous occasions when she would strain so hard to lean out of the window that it could only have been sheer luck that prevented her from falling right out. This intrusive, aggravating behaviour continued for some time, until one day the Devil decided he had had enough and was going to seek his revenge.

He waited patiently for her to settle at the window one night and when she stuck her head out, he wasted no time in unleashing his curse upon her and, in a flash, a gigantic set of horns had appeared on her head. After coming to her senses she desperately tried to pull her head back in through the window but was prevented from doing so by the horns. So she had no alternative but to stay put until the curse had worn off and, by all accounts, this took a very long time!

A Bad Night's Sleep

This account is also reported to have happened at the aforementioned property, High Street North, Olney. A new lodger had moved into the house that was reputed to be, a gentle man with a good clean conscience, a stout heart and a strong nerve.

One evening just as he was retiring to bed he noticed that the curtains in his bedroom weren't drawn properly as the moon was shining in and on his face. He went over to the window, fixed the curtains and returned to bed. No sooner was he back in his bed; he noticed that the curtains had moved again. Once again he got out of bed and went back to the window. This time, just as he was about to draw the curtains, he noticed the Devil sitting in a chair by the window. Now there is no doubt that most of us would have jumped, screamed or shouted at this, but no, not this gentleman who, totally unfazed by this evil presence, continued to close the curtains and went straight back to bed.

According to the legend, the devil was in a playful mood that night and repeated the game several times; however, the gentleman's perseverance paid off and he was finally left alone to get some sleep.- a case of goodness overcoming evil perhaps?

The Final Exit

This legend shows how the people of Olney joined forces, outwitted and finally banished the Devil from the Town for good.
A very unsavoury person by the name of John Faustus had begun to frequent one of the public houses in Olney. His visits were both menacing and frightening and not only did he make the landlord of the time act the fool whenever he wanted him to, he also behaved in an overbearing and sinister manner towards the other customers. As his visits increased, custom quickly decreased and people went to drink elsewhere. The landlord was beginning to despair, not only was he losing his customers, his livelihood was also being threatened - he was at his wit's end!

However, the evil goings on at the pub had not passed un-noticed by residents of the Town, who by now had begun to realise what they were up against. So with extreme care and caution, they hatched a crafty plan to get rid of the Devil once and for all.

Thirteen priests, armed with a bell, a bible and a candle, set off one night to look for Faustus. They didn't have to travel far because he was in his usual spot in the pub. On arrival, one of the priests stepped forward and asked Faustus if he would give the good people of Olney a respite from his actions for 100 years. Faustus replied that he felt such a request was excessive and couldn't possibly agree to it. Undaunted by the response, another of the priests stepped forward and asked Faustus if he would post-pone his visits until the candle he was holding burnt out. Faustus was caught off guard and agreed to the request without giving it sufficient thought. With this the wily old priest wasted no time and seized the opportunity of blowing out the candle, and to everyone's surprise and relief Faustus had disappeared.

The candle the priests had used was placed in the bottom of the pub's well and leg-end has it, that if this candle was ever found and re-lit, his visits would begin all over again....

Olney's First Church

The Parish Church of St Peter & St Paul was built at the turn of the 13th century to replace a much earlier church rumoured to have stood at the northerly end of the Town, roughly where the Castle Public House now stands.
The exact location of the earlier church is still something of a mystery as no remains have ever been found, nor is there any evidence to support its existence. Nevertheless, there are those who still maintain that this was the approximate site of the earlier church.

Some Local Influences and Local Theories

Yardley Road was originally called White Cross Hill. Why was this? Was it because the cross from the nearby church could be seen as you walked up this hill? Then there is the Whirly Pits, along Wellingborough Road, which are also referred to locally as " The Horse Pond ". Could this have been the spot where horses were left whilst their own-ers went to the church?, both are possibilities.
Also, there was a very large tree, the "**Churchyard Elm**", (referred to in more detail further on) which was situated in this area, also provides another clue.
Then there are the Feoffee Houses on Dartmouth Road, which have a strange tale associated with them. Workmen laying the foundation stones for the new houses uncovered a large quantity of bones. If this is to be believed, then could this area pos-sibly have been the graveyard for the church? It is difficult to confirm such an account as there are no documents held in the local records office confirming such a find.

It seems unlikely now that the first church of Olney will never be found. There has been so much redevelopment in the area and there is little demand to pursue a search in view of the disruption it would cause. And yet maybe there is still some faint hope. There is another area in the vicinity - Christian Wells field opposite the Queen Hotel in Dartmouth Road, which has been dormant for many years but looks likely to be developed in the near future. Could this unearth some new evidence perhaps?

Finally, the following fable describes an incident that is rumoured to have taken place in Lordship Close around the 1300's.

A Mysterious Goings-on...

The old Church that stood at the northerly end of the town had become very dilapidated and the Town was faced with a dilemma. Should they repair it or should they build a new one? The latter option was chosen and plans for a new church were drawn up.Finally it was decided to build the new church in a field in Lordship Close, which is at the southerly end of the Town, near the bridge.

After one heavy day's work laying the foundation stones, the builders left the site and returned home. The following morning when they arrived back at the site they were amazed to find an empty field. The stones they had laid the day before had been moved during the night and set out in a similar formation in a neighbouring field. Thinking it was just a joke being played on them, the builders moved the stones back to the designated field and continued with their work. Although the following morning they had the same experience. All the stones had been moved yet again to the neighbouring field and laid out as before. This time the builders were definitely not amused, especially as they had achieved virtually nothing after two days hard labouring. Thinking this was probably some cunning ploy by one of the locals, the builders decided to appoint a night watchman and they gave him strict instructions to stay awake, patrol the area regularly and to report any suspicious behaviour immediately.

The next morning the builders arrived to find that the stones had again been moved to the adjoining site. The appointed watchman was adamant that he had done all that had been asked of him and, as far as he was concerned, the night had passed uneventfully. He couldn't believe what he saw when dawn broke he could offer no logical explanation. The builders had little alternative but to believe him and the only conclusion they could all come to was that it had been the work of the Devil and they therefore decided to leave site straight away without moving the stones back.

A few years later, new builders were employed and the Church was built, uneventfully, around 1325'ish.

Great Trees

"The Druids performed their sacred rituals in the groves of the Oak and ever since it's had a central place in folklore".

Local trees

Olney and some of the surrounding villages have over the years been blessed with some very large and impressive trees. Many of these trees had their own names and were so distinctive that they were used as landmarks around the neighbouring countryside. Also, they have been recorded through time by some of Olney's more notable residents such as William Cowper, the poet, and Thomas Wright, past curator of the Cowper and Newton Museum, Olney.

Some of the Town's older residents will no doubt remember some of these trees, not least the *"Churchyard Elm"*, which came down about 40 years ago when the Dutch elm disease was rampant throughout the country. Much of the wood from these trees was salvaged and made into furniture or souvenirs - as well as providing kindling and logs for the stoves and fires. With the exception of one, *Gog* as mentioned below, which although still in place is now dead, all the others have gone and unfortunately their pictures do not capture their true size, or their magic.

However, like all countryside towns, Olney's trees are very much part of its heritage and to record the legends surrounding some of them, serves as a reminder to newer residents the contribution made to the Town's past by its rich natural resources.

Their Location

The Churchyard Elm

Site: Olney: Dartmouth Road, where the bus stop now stands.
Info: In 1893 Thomas Wright dated this tree to be at least 600 years old. If this is correct, and, if the tree did backdate to around 1293, this was approximately the same period, when the first Church of Olney was deemed to have stood in this vicinity and the name given to the tree would also give credence to the legend.

The size and spread of the Churchyard Elm provided a decent shelter and even a comfortable resting place for residents and travellers alike. It finally came down around 1950 and the bus shelter was erected on the spot in 1977 to commemorate Queen Elizabeth's Silver Jubilee.

Cowper's Oak

Site: On private land in Weston Underwood.
Info: Cowper's Oak, had a girth of 22ft 6ins, and was a favourite retreat for William Cowper when he sought inspiration and the tranquillity of the surrounding countryside. Regrettably the tree burnt down in 1950.

"And when the thousand years have ended, Satan will be loosened from his prison and will come out to deceive the nations which are at the four corners of the earth, that is Gog and Magog to gather them for battle".

Revelation, Ch. 20 Vs7-8

Gog

Site: Private land, Yardley Hastings
Info: This was the largest of all the trees – with a girth of 32ft - it stands in a field named in its honour Gog Field. Although now dead and with no branches on its irregular shaped trunk, what's left of it is a menacing sight and it sticks out of the ground like an enormous rotten tooth.

Magog

Site: Private land, Yardley Hastings
Info: No longer standing today, this tree was possibly the oldest of them all and was rumoured to have been planted by Lady Judith, niece of the Earl of Waltheof. It stood 50 yards distant from Gog and was blessed with a regular trunk and a girth of 29 feet. The last leaf was seen about 1960 around the same time as the tree was felled.

Some old English customs and associations

A great protector

The oak tree was a great protector against lightning.

The ageing process

If you carried an acorn in your pocket it would slow down the ageing process.

Toothache

If you suffered from toothache, relief could be found by driving a nail into the trunk of the tree.

The Oakmen

Centuries ago it was believed that the saplings that sprouted from the Oak tree were the homes of small and unpleasant creatures called Oakmen. These pixie-like creatures were tricksters who had a nasty and sinister side to them. One of their favourite tricks was to offer a passing traveller delicious, mouth-watering food, which in reality, was a poisonous fungus whose appearance had been disguised by their magic.

Battle on The Bridge 1643

During the reign of Charles 1st **(1625 - 1649)** and following a Scottish Invasion, an Irish Rebellion and a conflict between the King and Parliament, war broke out.

In the early hours of Sunday **4th November 1643**, the King's forces, led by Prince Rupert, marched into Olney to attack the Parliamentarians, who were stationed locally under the guard of Col E. Harvey. Within 15 minutes of the alarm being raised, the King's troops were fast approaching the Town and making their way down Yardley Road. An extensive, fierce, and bloody battle followed, with fighting in and around Olney, and Sherington. It even managed to reach the bridge at Newport Pagnell.

Olney Bridge from an early engraving.

The Parliamentarians mustered for one last stand against the Royal troops on the bridge at Olney but there were many casualties, both dead and injured. Triumphant in their attack, the King's forces departed post haste, leaving Olney to recover and return to normal.

Evidence of the battle has surfaced from time to time when work has been carried out on land and in the river around the area. A sword and other military artefacts so discovered and dating back to the period are now on display – with many other items of local interest - in the Gordon Osborn Room at the Cowper & Newton Museum.

Battle on the Bridge.

Some of Olney's Humour

A Short Story, Cowper Press, 1907

Scene: Hallelujah Lamp Post, Olney

Cyclist: Can you kindly tell me how far it is to Fenny Stratford?

Olneyite: It's about the same distance to Fenny Stratford as it is to everywhere else from here. It's about twelve miles to Fenny Stratford, 12 miles to Stony Stratford, 12 miles to Northampton, 12 miles to Bedford, 12 miles to Wellingborough, 12 miles to Heaven and 12 miles to Hell.

Cyclist: Then you Olneyites have not travelled far....

Is there some sense in this maybe?

Today Fenny Stratford is 13.2 miles, Stony Stratford 13.1 miles, Wellingborough 11.3miles, Bedford 12.1 miles and Northampton is 13.8 miles....

The Great Fire of Olney, 1854. The London Illustrated News.

Great Fires of Olney

Great Fires of Olney

"Its menacing presence was always there. It was just watching and waiting patiently for the right opportunity to strike. When, without a moments notice, a great phoenix rose up from the ashes and began spreading its wings of mass destruction rapidly over the residents of Olney".

Candles, gas lamps, thatched cottages, alcohol, even arsonists have all contributed to the many fires over the years, all of which were abundantly available preceding the fires. Many historical records have been lost and destroyed both in, and since these fires, but with the help of past authors and local poets we are able to get some idea of what actually happened when the fires struck.

Dates of some of Olney's more notable fires, (recorded ones).

1.	1777	8 properties destroyed
2.	1783	several properties destroyed
3.	1786	43 houses destroyed
4.	1853	3 deaths from fires
5.	1854	Great fire of Olney, 80 properties damaged
6.	1878	Old Mill burns down, first time
7.	1887	3 properties destroyed
8.	1907	fire at the Gasworks
9.	1928	Cowley fire
10.	1965	Cowper Memorial Church
11.	1965	Old Mill finally burns down

October 1777

The poet William Cowper recorded one of the earliest fires in the Town. He describes a night when 7 to 8 properties in Olney caught fire and had the wind been any higher, many more would have gone up in flames. The losses from this fire amounted to £450, which was not covered by insurance; but after heavy campaigning by the Reverend John Newton, residents - the poor as well as the better off – all gave generously and the Town managed to raise sufficient money to help those afflicted.

November 1783

It was a bitterly cold but calm Saturday night in November, the hour was late and most people had gone to bed. Even William Cowper was snugly tucked up when, " Fire! Fire!" was bellowed up his staircase by an unknown party. William jumped out of bed and dashed to the window where he saw fire coming from the roof of his neighbour, Mr Palmer. After realising that he was not in immediate danger he quickly got dressed and went to help.

The fire had spread rapidly via the thatched roofs and in next to no time it had reached the adjoining properties of George Griggs and the Tyrell residence. By now most of the town was awake; and fear and panic was spreading with the same intensity as the fire.

Thick black smoke poured onto the Market Place, markedly reducing visibility, and much screaming, crying; coughing, choking and retching could also be clearly heard. Many took advantage of the situation by looting and helping themselves to anything they could find, especially food and drink, even ironmongery. Alcohol seemed to be flowing freely and there was much drunkenness; however, the more honest residents of the Town rallied round and helped those whose properties had been affected by the fire by helping them move their possessions to place of safe-keeping. One of these safe havens was Orchard Side (now the Museum), which was reported as being full to capacity within two hours of the fire starting.

In all the confusion and chaos, Mr Griggs suffered a hat-trick of tragedies. It really wasn't his night. Not only was his house on fire, but he also mistakenly gave 18 guineas for safekeeping to a complete stranger whom he mistook for his wife. After realising his mistake, he turned back to his house only to see to his horror £40 worth of wool going up in flames. The fire was finally brought under control after numerous buckets of water had been applied - stopping just 6 yards short of Daniel Raban's woodpile.

The cause of the fire was later put down to arson. A tar barrel and a quantity of tallow stored in the back garden of one of the properties had been deliberately set on fire. There are no records of anyone being brought to justice for starting the fire but many people were severely reprimanded for their behaviour that night.

Follow-on from the Fire of November 1783

Two un-named women and a boy received justice.

Sue Riviss - caught stealing a piece of beef.

She claimed she was only looking after it and refused to hand it over despite several requests to do so and so she was eventually forced to the ground and the beef was taken from her. Where the meat came from and to whom it belonged nobody knew, although at her trial Daniel Raban (the baker's son) made a plea on her behalf and she was spared from going to County Jail.

Molly Boswell's sons - caught stealing Mr Griggs' ironmongery.

These cheeky boys stole ironmongery from right under the very nose of Mr Griggs whilst his house was on fire.

Fires in Olney 1852 – 1853

For some months, Olney suffered a spate of nocturnal robberies and fires. No one was ever caught or tried for the crimes but the Town was terrorized for many long and wearisome months.

The first of the fires began on **Christmas Eve 1852**, around 10.30 pm when Mr Whitmee's large barley stack, situated on the Lavendon Road, was set alight. Fortunately for him, and with the commendable effort of the townsfolk, they quickly managed to extinguish the fire which saved about a third of the stack; whilst the remaining two thirds were covered by insurance.

The following Monday an attempt was made to set fire to the premises of Miss Raban, a tenant of a farm belonging to Lord Dartmouth. This time the fire was quickly put out before any real damage could be done and again insurance covered the losses.

A few days later, on **New Year's Eve** around 7 pm, when most people were preparing to celebrate the evening's festivities, fire broke out in the large barn belonging to the local butcher, Thomas Soul.
The barn housed many animals - cows, pigs, and horses - all of which were kept under the charge of Joseph Palmer. The fire spread rapidly and the cries from the trapped animals were horrendous, there was no time to save any of them. The scene was tragic and the mournful moans from the animals as they burned were too much for some to bear and they had to leave. But for those that did stay, the memory of that night remained with them for a very long time afterwards.

When the fire was finally put out, the full extent of the damage could be seen. The small thatched hovels that housed some of the smaller animals had been totally destroyed. The main barn, where the majority of the animals had been kept, was burnt to a cinder and the charred remains of animals, some still tethered, continued smouldering for many hours afterwards. It was a heart rendering scene that didn't end there.

On Sunday **2nd January**, another attempt was made to fire the barns belonging to the Soul family. Fortunately the arsonist was not successful but by now the entire town was in a great state of agitation. Night watchmen were appointed and placed in strategic areas around the Town to keep a look out for any suspicious behaviour and this seemed to work for a while - until....

Tuesday **4th January**, when the cow barn behind the Bakehouse, High Street South was set on fire. This time the fire caught hold of the building quickly and destroyed the old Bakehouse within a matter of minutes. The fire then spread to the house of Mr Killingsworth, the local watchmaker, and quickly moved on to adjoining properties. It was relentless in its mission and many feared that the devastation would spread further up the High Street. Furniture and other possessions were removed from twelve nearby properties and the fire was eventually brought under control.

But it didn't end there. One of the burning barns to the rear of Mr Killingsworth's house had collapsed and a burning mass of rubble had fallen on the helpers. One, Jacob Clifton, was trapped beneath it, and it proved extremely difficult to reach him; but rescue him they did, albeit in a badly injured state, and he was given urgent medical attention. John Marson, the local rat catcher, was later found burned and mutilated beyond recognition and his body was taken straight to the Church. By 9 pm the fire had been brought under control and many retuned to their homes dirty, worn out and in shock from the night's events.

At 9 o'clock the next morning, a bellman was dashing around the town frantically ringing his bell and shouting for the whereabouts of William Scott, a local farmer's son, who had not been seen since the night of the fire.

" If anyone knows of his whereabouts would they please come forward. His family is deeply worried that something has happened to him. Please help, please look for William Scott".

Many heard the plea and some clearly remembered having seen William helping at the fire and so a search was made of the burnt out site. His body was eventually found and in the same spot as John Marson but buried much, much deeper; the fire had barely touched his clothes, yet his hands and face were missing.

News of these fires was now beginning to attract national attention and the two insurance companies in the Town had started restricting payments. Everybody in Olney seemed to be affected in one way or another. Olney had an arsonist in its midst, one that needed to be caught quickly, and before he or she could strike again.

The Home Office sent three active officers from Scotland Yard and a reward of £200 was offered; so too was a free pardon for the culprit by Her Majesty the Queen. Although some of the residents had decided to take the matter into their own hands and wrote a public letter to the arsonist, which was widely and heavily displayed throughout certain areas of the Town.

Thorough investigations were carried out and certain people were interviewed and questioned. Many suspected who the arsonist was but there was never sufficient evidence, and so nobody was ever apprehended.

INCENDIARY FIRES.

Whereas certain evil-disposed persons having maliciously, from some cause at present unknown, destroyed by **FIRE** the property of several Inhabitants of **OLNEY** and neighbourhood ; and information of the same having been forwarded to the proper quarter, with a view to bringing the culprits guilty of such atrocious crimes to condign punishment, it is resolved, preparatory to the adoption of severe measures, to make the following

APPEAL TO THE INHABITANTS.

WORKING MEN,

THROUGHOUT the country the woeful tidings have spread, that the ASSASSIN-LIKE CRIME OF INCENDIARISM is taking deep-root amongst the once loyal and well-disposed people of OLNEY,—rendering the mention of you "a bye word and a reproach," and that a fearful system of terror reigns amongst your neighbours, lest whilst reposing in their beds, some midnight prowler should lurk unseen about their houses, and "on fiendish purposes bent," suddenly light up a conflagration, which might destroy not only their worldly possessions, but the lives of those they hold most dear.

Contemplate solemnly, my friends, such deeds in their manifold horrors—view the frightful ruin and loss of life wrought thereby (directly and indirectly) amongst your unoffending fellow creatures, look upward, and think of the eye of an all-seeing, evil-hating, and sin-punishing God—and under the empire of sober reason, consider WHAT GOOD CAN RESULT THEREFROM to any of you? None at all : rather as "your sins will find you out," so will Providence unerringly bring you to judgment—either in this world or in that which is to come.

Are you in distress from low wages, or oppressed by any one ? Burning your neighbours' property, and placing their lives in jeopardy, will prove no remedy. Without removing a single grievance, you will be only adding to the distress of the country. Rather exercise your privilege as free-born Englishmen, and as members of a civilised Christian community, proclaim in public meeting, the extent of your sufferings, where those disposed to assist you will have an opportunity of knowing your wants, and of alleviating them.

By the dastardly underhand machinations of a midnight incendiary, you can never expect to thrive. To your upright sentiments as husbands—as affectionate fathers and brothers—to your loyalty as British Citizens —to your pride, as the rational producers, and not the insane destroyers of wealth—by the love you bear to your wives and little ones—by the enthusiasm of your English hearts, that once burned so highly on the altar of your country (if history speaks true), and sent forth a Nelson whose motto was, "England expects every man will do his duty," "in that state of life in which it has pleased God to call him;" and, above all, by the hope that you may on your dying bed receive mercy as you have shown mercy, this appeal is made to your better feelings—asking your aid to stop the evil, and cast out the offenders.

Hereafter, should this prove in vain, those watching in secret, will at the proper moment when least expected, denounce openly to offended justice the guilty delinquents.

And lastly, to one and all of the inhabitants of Olney, I would say, **Arouse yourselves from your supineness, and protect your property and your persons by an efficient Police force, before it be too late.**

Your friend and fellow-labourer,

Jan. 8th, 1853.   **A WORKING MAN.**

A public plea to Olney's arsonist 1853.

A few nights later, on **January 29th**, an attempt was made to light a fire at the stables of Lodge Farm, the home of Mr Higgins, but it was soon spotted and put out. The cause this time was put down to three drunken strangers who had been seen in the Weston Underwood area making a nuisance of themselves that night.

These three had continued their rowdy outbursts until they reached the White Lion at Stoke Goldington, where they were arrested and given a sentence of three months' hard labour for all the trouble they had caused.

But the fires still persisted and the barns belonging to Mr Higgins were targeted again and this time a straw stack was completely burnt down. Then events took a strange turn, several curious and anonymous letters were sent to Mr Soul jun. & Co. Olney, which read -:

" Behold! The days of vengeance, famine, fire
and pestilence, sword & co, what will become of
all the glass when all fool perish like grass".

Even with all the spelling mistakes and the reference to grass, no one had the faintest idea what it meant. The police suspected a known fanatic in London and so the matter was never treated too seriously, but the letters were kept by the police as evidence. Sadly, the incidents of the fires had caused Mrs Soul great distress and she died at an early age in February 1853.

Jacob Clifton, who had suffered the terrible injuries in the fire on **January 4th**, was a stonemason by trade, and one that had a large family to support. His family began to despair when it was realised that Jacob would have to spend the remainder of his life in a wheelchair when a family friend, *All hands to the pumps.*
Thomas Revis, and a few others came to their rescue by raising funds for them around the Town.

Olney then had a break from the fires for a short while and life in the Town began to get back to normal – but alas, not for long. On the **March 29th** at 6 pm, a fire broke out again at the home of Mr Higgins and, this time, a wheat hovel was completely destroyed.

Two weeks later, around 3pm, the cry of " Fire!" was heard coming from a cottage in Bridge Street. The fire had set light to three thatched roofs but had found a temporary respite at Miss Raban's house, which had a tiled roof. Unfortunately though, it did not stop there - the embers carried by the wind had set alight two more thatched cottages. Fire engines arrived at the scene and before long the fire was brought safely under control.

This time the fire had been started quite by accident. A passing steam engine which had been working nearby was blamed, the sparks from its chimney had set fire to the thatches as it had passed .

Though the terrible irony of this disaster was that one of the houses destroyed by the fire had belonged to William Scott, the young man who had died tragically in Mr Killingsworth's fire.

The death count from the fires over the year rose to three. Jacob Clifton did not survive for very long and John Marson, William Scott and Jacob are all remembered and honoured in a Ballard written about the fires in 1853 by Thomas Aspray. This Ballard was printed and heavily distributed throughout the Town as was sold for the benefit of the bereaved families.

The Great Fire of Olney 1854

Less than a year later Olney suffered its worst fire to date. Around 2 o'clock one afternoon fire broke out at the northernly end of the High Street in a small washhouse to the rear of Daniel Morgan's, the Grocer. The fire spread quickly onto the business next door and the house rapidly disintegrated under the weight of the flames. In next to no time the strong wind had blown sparks down, and on to the roof of Mr Covington's, the Blacksmith, which was on the opposite side of the High Street.

The fire rapidly spread across the thatched rooftops of neighbouring houses and suddenly some 30 houses on the eastern side of the High Street were on fire, as well as a dozen more on the western side. Furniture and possessions were frantically removed from the houses and stacked in the street but the flying embers soon turned them into an enormous bonfire, nowhere seemed safe, everywhere was ablaze.

Three fire engines soon arrived at the scene, two from Newport Pagnell and one from Yardley Hastings. The firemen strove bravely and tirelessly to control the fires and water was pumped from neighbouring wells and from the Whirly Pits; but it was a fruitless effort and many residents could only look on helplessly, watching their properties disintegrate in front of them.

The cause though accidental had rendered nearly 300 people homeless, and many were forced to leave the Town whilst other residents were left with nothing other than the clothes they were wearing. A number of women and children were housed temporarily in the National School whilst others were taken in by their neighbours, which left the remaining balance with no other choice but to sleep outside.

In total, 55 properties burnt to the ground and 25 were seriously damaged but miraculously there was no loss of life. The loss from the fire was estimated between £9 - £10,000 but insurance only covered losses to the value of £3,000. The fire was reported in numerous newspapers and the London Illustrated News sent a reporter to capture the scene and record the events. After the article was printed, gifts of food and clothing came flooding in to the Town.

Stanza on the Fire of Olney January 4th, 1853

We've had a proof convincing, grave,
In Olney's late disaster:
That fire although a useful slave
Is always a bad master.

For long, long years to Mister Soul
It was a servant true;
It bak'd his pastry (twist and roll)
And warmed his household too.

But now the rebel blazes out,
Like dragon from a dungeon:
Nor heeds the rushing water spout
Played on him by the engine.

Its face of flame glowed from the thatch
Its red teeth at the door:
It snapped the roof like a match,
And hurled it to the floor.

Then to a neighbouring dwelling fled,
And tasted human blood:
And roared and roll'd as broad and red
As a volcanic flood.

The firmament seem'd set on fire,
The stars all died away:
The river near, the hills and spire
Shone out as clear as day.

It shadowed forth that fire of old,
That half consumed the town:
Or conflagration fierce and bold
That burns a forest down.

It filled the vale with sparks and smoke,
And sudden shrieks of women;
Then vanished in a sable cloak,
Like any other demon.

Who is the cruel wicked one
That all this misery made?
Walks he beneath the blessed sun,
Or lurks he in the shade?

Incendiary, thy darkest den,
Justice divine will light:
And reckon with thee for the men,
Who perished in that night.

Thomas Aspray

Fire at Olney Mill 1878

In 1876 Charles Henry Whitworth purchased the Olney Mill with a grand expansion plan in mind. He aimed to make the Olney Mill one of the most efficient and powerful watermills in the area. But after spending several thousands of pounds on the refurbishment on Thursday 3rd January 1878, a familiar cry of "Fire!" was heard coming from the river area. Many rushed initially towards the Church but soon witnessed the Mill raging fiercely away.

Willing helpers desperately and bravely tried to rescue some of the stock but were beaten back by the flames. The lift then caught fire and within a short space of time the Mill was a raging inferno. The Olney Fire appliances were the first to arrive at the scene; and whilst the fire was being fought, nearby properties had their contents removed and dampened down. At 11.20pm an engine from Newport Pagnell arrived and with the combined forces they managed to save the adjoining properties but the Mill carried on burning throughout the night.

By 8.30am the following morning the last of the fire engines left the Mill. It was a pitiful scene. The Mill with its charred and blackened façade made a very sorry sight for Olney and charred pieces of wood had been reported being seen as far away as Lavendon.

The fire at the Mill was the last straw for the Town and a mass public meeting was called to demand the updating of the inadequate and obsolescent fire service. Eight months later the Olney Fire Brigade was formed with 12 volunteers who gave their time and services freely and they even paid for their own uniforms.

November 14th 1.30 pm 1882

A large carpenters shop at the back of Mr Frederick Smith's caught fire and, because of the high wind and the combustible nature of the contents, nothing could be saved.

October 2nd 1887

The Baptist Chapel was conducting a service when the church doors flew open and the cry of "Fire!" was heard - three cottages in the Leys had caught fire. The congregation began to panic and started to stampede towards the doors but the Pastor, remaining cool and collected, calmed his flock and prevented a possible disaster. The Fire Brigade attended but was unable to save the burning properties and they were ultimately demolished.

Lot 18.

(Colored Green on Plan).

The Olney Mills

situate on the Ouse close to the Town, comprising the substantial stone built and slated

FLOUR MILLS

of five floors with large undershot water and other wheels and shafting and pulleys throughout, exhaust trunk and spouts. On the

GROUND FLOOR—3 pairs of Stones, Dynamo, Set of Elevators from bottom to top of Mill; on the

FIRST FLOOR—6 roller mills, 7 reductions, 2 pairs of stones, bean splitters. Set of 18 rolls and
    wheat cleaning plant;

SECOND FLOOR—Exhaust Fans and Purifiers, Dickey Sieves, Offal Mill, sieves, bins and tank.

THIRD FLOOR—7 Centrifugals and 2 Mixers;

TOP FLOOR—Flour Mixer, Bell driven Friction Hoist, and two Grové Rotaries.

The Engine House with 40 h.p. gas engine by Grice, with hand pump. Boiler House, Coal Store.

The contiguous range of buildings include, Office, Stabling for 7 horses, 2 Loose Boxes, 4-bay Wagon
    Sheds, Stores and lofts, Motor Garage.

In the rear is the Cattle Yard with Cow Shed for five, 6-bay Open Shed, Cow House and Shed.

The Attractive Residence

contains on the

GROUND FLOOR—Tiled Entrance Hall, Drawing Room 18ft. × 16ft., Dining Room 15ft. × 14ft.,
    (these rooms are believed to have fire places from the old Manor House), Kitchen, Scullery with
    copper, Pantry, Larder and Cellar.

FIRST FLOOR—4 Bedrooms, Bath Room, and W.C.

SECOND FLOOR—2 Bedrooms and Box Room.

THE OLD WORLD GROUNDS

are those of the old Manor House and are particularly choice, they are skirted by the Ouse and
finely timbered, having lawns and flower beds and borders, greenhouse and tool house.

VEGETABLE AND FRUIT GARDEN

walled-in with good varieties of fruit trees, shrubs and plants. Near is the

QUAINT OLD FASHIONED COTTAGE

of 6 rooms with washhouse and

LARGE WALLED-IN GARDEN.

There is a cob in the river, 2 boat houses, dam and flood gates, the whole covers an area of about

48 acres.

principally rich Ouse Meadows.

Cowley Fire 1928

Messrs. S. Cowley Ltd, Boot and Shoe Manufacturers, Clickers Yard, Yardley Road had begun life in two small cottages elsewhere in the Town but the business flourished and by 1916 had expanded to such an extent that more space was required. A new factory was built in Clickers Yard and within another ten years, the company was employing a full time staff of nearly 200.

At 9am one typically lazy, quiet Sunday morning Mr Cowley's gardener, Mr Freeman, decided to have a bonfire to burn some grass cuttings that were in the back garden of Mr Cowley's house. Little did Mr Freeman know that this small act would end up in the history books as one Olney's worst disasters.

Rescuing the stock.

Mr Freeman had lit the bonfire in a slightly different place than normal but he was happy with its progress so went off to the house to pump some water. On his return, he was horrified to see that sparks from the bonfire had ignited the nearby box shed, which was now burning away fiercely. The shed contained paper and boxes and, despite the desperate efforts of the gardener and by now Mr Cowley too, there was no hope of controlling the fire. The flames then spread to the adjoining factory and many of its workers and other willing helpers frantically removed goods and chattels from the nearby cottages to safer places; inevitably damaging some of these in the process.

The Olney Fire Brigade quickly arrived at the scene but soon discovered that their once again outdated fire appliances were incapable of coping with a fire of such magnitude. The main hose leaked and the manual pump, which took 18 people to work, was unable to make any significant impact on the fire. The Newport Pagnell Fire Brigade and Wolverton Rail Brigade arrived and, with more powerful appliances they were able to pump water from the nearby Whirly Pits.

Within two hours of the fire starting, the factory that once employed nearly 200 people had been razed to the ground. Its modern machinery had been twisted into fantastic shapes and 3000 pairs of boots and shoes had been burnt to a cinder. Although 5000 pairs of boots and shoes were saved, the net damage was estimated at £30,000 and, with insufficient finances available, the factory was never rebuilt.

Remains of the factory.

The Olney Rail Station, Midland Road, Olney.

Trams
and
Trains

Olney Tramline

During **1875** and shortly after the failed attempt to establish a rail link between Olney and Newport Pagnell, it was still felt that a rail link or tramway was needed to connect the two towns and other villages together. The only form of public transport currently available was a horse drawn bus owned and run by a Mrs Fontaine of the Swan Hotel, Newport Pagnell, but this bus had seen better days it was worn out, slow, and unreliable.

A bit closer to home the Wolverton Railway Carriage Works, Wolverton had built a tramline similar to that suggested for Olney and it had been working well for some time. With this in mind, the townsfolk preferred the tramline as the viable option for Olney and Newport Pagnell.

In 1887 a group of businessmen met and a consortium was formed that wasted no time in drawing up an application to place before Parliament for the **1887** Newport Pagnell Tramways Act.

A series of meetings were held in the Towns and villages along the route, and having seen the advantages and benefits that would come with a tramline, the majority residents wholeheartedly supported the scheme. A meeting held in the National School in Olney on Thursday **28th January 1888**, saw a resolution passed approving the scheme, and in September that year work began on the line.

However, problems soon became apparent and, after 13 years of battling with numerous issues, not least with the Bridge Trustees along the route plus the many stringent rules and regulations that had to be adhered to, the problems with contractors and the continual cash flow difficulties, the project was abandoned; and the track already laid was taken up and the roads were restored by Bucks County Council.

So why did the scheme fail?

There were a number of contributing factors and the following outlines some of them in more detail.

1. Money

As with most infra-structural development schemes, money appeared to be the biggest obstacle. The scheme in its day was very expensive to construct and it was heavily reliant upon local resources. Those that had agreed to invest were ultra cautious, many had suffered substantial losses from the failure of the rail link between Newport Pagnell and Olney, which had been partially constructed a few years previously, and were very wary of a repeat performance. This over-cautious approach though discouraged new investors and the scheme was in a continuing day-to-day cash flow crisis. In addition to this and following complaints from residents that the engines of the proposed trams would generate too much noise as they passed through the Towns and villages, (as the engines were steam driven) the Tramline Company agreed initially to substitute them for electric trams. However, when reviewing this decision at a later date, they realised it was an expensive option and one that would increase the overheads to such a capacity that the scheme would not be viable...

2. The Bridge

The first bridge out of Town of Olney was known as the Duchy Bridge; at the time of the tramline construction this bridge was in a dilapidated state and desperately in need of repair. The Trustees of the Bridge well aware of its condition and placed near impossible demands upon the Tramline Company for its restoration. After some years of debate and argument, no resolution to the problem could be found, although it was proposed by the Tramway Company to place an iron girder bridge alongside the original bridge.
At Sherington Bridge the Tramway Company had constructed an iron girder frame on the west side of the bridge to take the track, but it had caused a public outcry.

3. Too Narrow

The road entering the town of Olney was found to be too narrow at High Street South; it needed to be widened to accommodate the track. One particular property that presented it self as a bit of a problem was, No 9 High Street South, now The Wine Bar. This was a bakery business at the time, owned by a Mr D N Morgan and it was his property that was obstructing the proposed route of the track. Negotiations were made to purchase and demolish the property, but before this could be completed the Tramway project collapsed.

4. Track Trouble

The proposed laying of the track through the village of Emberton caused a serious problem and turned out to be the final nail in the coffin of the Tramway Company. The Board of Trade refused to allow the line to go through the village, stating, that the bends in the road were too sharp for a tram to negotiate. An alternative solution was found but it meant the tramline would cross land owned by a farmer who unfortunately was in bad health and in no fit state to enter into any agreement.

The Tramway Company when applying to Parliament for their Act had failed to insert a clause of compulsory purchase over private land as they thought the route of the tramline could and would be accommodated on roads or verges. Later the Emberton by-pass was constructed on the route the Tramway Company wanted to use and this was the final and insurmountable problem, which brought work on the project to a standstill.

5. And Finally

In **February 1892**, nearly 13 years after the scheme was started, Bucks County Council now doubted whether the tramline could ever be finished so they issued the Tramline Company with an ultimatum. If the project was not completed by the **1st June 1893**, the track already laid and associated materials would be removed and the stock would be sold to recoup any losses in making the roads good again where track had been removed. June came and went, and in **November 1892**, the Tramline Company went into liquidation and Bucks County Council kept to their word and the scheme became moribund.

The Olney Train Station

Olney's train station was on the Northampton / Bedford link line and was situated at the northern end of the Town at the bottom of Midland Road, in an area that has since been re-developed. The station was built in **1870** and was run by the Midland Rail Company who opened it for business on the **10th June 1872**.

By **1907** the Midland Rail Company was employing the following staff at Olney's station.

Station Master	R. Grice
Senior Clerk	A. Crosley
Booking Clerk	C. Harris
Machine Clerk	H. Field
Station Porters	C. Sizer and C.E. Pearce
Assistant Porter	P. Porter
Goods Checker	G. Horn
Signal Men	G. Prince and T. Sarson

The station was closed in 1963 (as part of the Beeching plan) and the track was removed and the building was later demolished. The land was then sold for re-development and the bridge that crossed the river at Clifton Reynes was removed in the 1980s.

Demonstrating lace making outside the Viper Barn, Cowper and Newton Museum, Olney.

Olney Lace

Olney Lace
In the beginning....

Between the 14th and 15th centuries, Continental lace makers came to live in the North Bucks area as a result of religious persecution in their own countries. Lace makers from Lille and Mechlin settled in Olney and they taught the local ladies how to make bobbin lace. As a result of this instruction, a cottage industry gradually developed and went on to flourish in Olney for the next 300 years.

At the time William Cowper was residing at Orchard Side **(1768-1786)**, the population of Olney was just 2,500 of which about half (men, women and children) were employed in the lace making trade. Working conditions were tough and the work was extremely onerous, especially when considering the meagre pittance that was earned in return.

On the **8th July 1780**, William Cowper learnt of a new tax that was going to be imposed on the lace makers and, desperate to help them, he signed their objecting petition and also sent a letter to Mr J Hill at the Houses of Parliament expressing his thoughts and concerns over it.

"I am an eye witness of their poverty and do know that hundreds in this little town are upon the point of starving and that the most unremitting industry is barely sufficient to keep them from it".

Over time...

By the **1800s** the demand for hand-made lace was at an all time high in Olney and many women found themselves earning more money making lace than by working in the domestic market. But the hours were still long and hard and working between 10 and 12 hours a day left the women with little time for domestic chores.

The wife of a local vicar in the Olney area was reputed to have designed this beautiful border of the church towers and was made for Elizabeth Bumfrey in 1747.
Elizabeth was due to marry Sir John Dobbin but the wedding never took place, Elizabeth died of smallpox.
The border was found in the 1930's along with the bill of the sale and is now on display at the Cowper and Newton Museum.

Most of the lace makers could be found working in the small houses just off the Market Place and in Silver End, which was classed as the slum area of Olney; but with low wages of just 3 shillings per week, it was all they could afford-theirs was a pitiful existence. The dire living conditions also contributed to bad health. Many suffered from lung disease and tuberculosis, which was often seen in young females between the ages of 15 and 25. And, as if this wasn't enough, there were outbreaks of cholera and typhus in **1831** and **1849** when many people died, but for those that did survive they lived in constant fear.

By the **1850s** machine-made lace had been introduced and for a time Olney's trade remained stable. However, with this new machine-made lace being much, much, cheaper consumers began to switch, even though the hand-made product was superior in both looks and quality.

By the **1900s** some locals became dealers and locally made lace was sold via the larger markets and the London shops. It was a more profitable business for the dealers and they consequently enjoyed a more comfortable standard of living and were able to improve their housing conditions.

By the **1940s** the last of the main lace dealers, Harry Armstrong, had died and only a few in Olney continued making lace and this was mainly for personal consumption.

In the **1950s** and **1960s** there was a lace revival and with the help of the Womens Institute and Adult Education classes, the Olney Lace Circle was formed in 1979.

Lace is still being made in Olney but only on a modest scale. Some examples of fine lace making and the methods used can be seen in the Lace Exhibition at the Cowper and Newton Museum, it's well worth a visit.

A lace makers candle stool.

Bygone days
Lace Makers' Holiday: Tanders Day

Each year on the **30th November**, St Andrew's Day, Olney lace makers were allowed a day off from work to participate in the celebrations being held in the Town. Metheglin, a very strong mead-like drink, was consumed in vast amounts and, to soak up all the local brew, cakes made from caraway seeds were eaten in abundance.

Mr Cobb from Honey House, (No 24 High Street), was a beekeeper and carpenter by trade but had been given a special licence for St Andrew's Day, which allowed him to make this infamous brew. It was good stuff by all accounts and long queues eager to buy it could be seen stretching quite a distance down the High Street. But being such a strong drink, did have its consequences and there was many suffering from a hefty hangover the following day.

The festivities went on all day and well into the night and games were played such as "Jack be nimble, Jack be quick" and by all accounts much fun was had by all. The following day the lace makers were allowed to light the candles on their stools and the glass lobes that surrounded them gave much needed light for working during the forthcoming winter months. Over the years the name changed and St Andrew's Day became better known locally as Tanders Day.

The Tells....

Tells were rhymes without any literal meaning and the children were permitted to chant them whilst making their lace. Not only did it help alleviate the boredom but it was also allowed and tolerated because it kept the work rate constant.

Some of the Lace Sites

There are a number of very pretty, notable houses along the High Street, many of which have some very important historical connections with the bygone lace trade of Olney.

The Old Penny House: No. 22 High Street: A Dame School

In **1800** the Old Penny House was a Dame School, which was run by a Sarah Duxbury, and it was here that lace making could be learnt for a few extra pence per week. The girls were also taught how to read and write although the main emphasis was on how to make lace.

Girls as young as four would gather in a small room in the house, which had little or no heating and it was here that they were shown how to make lace. They were strict times for the girls and there were many rules and regulations to adhere to. One such example was long hair; this had to be tied back as loose hairs could get worked into the pattern. Necks and arms were to be kept bare for when punishment was administered, and it was not uncommon to hear of children having their heads pushed on to the lace pillows and their noses rubbed on the pins! – Ouch!

No.44 High Street: Training Academy

This was the home and training academy of the outstanding parchment designer, John Millward. John was credited with many designs between 1820 -1828 and continued wining awards until 1851. He was also credited with the design for the lace crowns for babies' caps, which later became better known as "Millward's Caps".

John Millwards reputation travelled as far as America where shipments of his work were sent regularly until the outbreak of the Civil War. The alleyway to the side of the house later became known as Millwards Entry and was the main entrance into the academy. Today the alleyway is better known as Millards Entry, the "w" having been dropped over the years.

The Cowper and Newton Museum

One of the many lace displays.

The Cowper and Newton Museum was also a lace factory for many years, which was run and managed by Mrs Langley, wife of the local vicar. Mrs Langley engaged the services of mistresses who assisted her with the rooms and with the supervising of the 40 lace makers that were employed. Some of the best work in the town was produced here and among their customers were Queen Adelaide, Lady Denbigh and the Marchioness of Northampton.

Influential People

Harry Armstrong was a colourful character and one who was full of life. He was one of the main lace dealers in the Town and one that made a valuable contribution to the lace industry in Olney. As well as having a good eye for business and potential opportunities, he was also a much-liked gentleman who treated his

Lace Factory

ladies with the utmost respect. Even today, Harry is a figurehead who is remembered with affection by the older residents of the Town.

Harry lived in a rented cottage in Stoke Goldington and it was here that he set up and ran the Bucks Cottage Workers' Agency. Harry would personally visit his ladies to deliver the materials and then collect the finished articles. He was also a designer and could therefore give advice and make suggestions for improvements. He was careful to maintain quality control by checking for defects because he was the one who dealt directly with the buyers in the larger markets and the London shops. By **1911** Buckinghamshire lace had become world famous and the Bucks Cottage Workers Agency was awarded a Gold medal at the Empire and Imperial Exhibition in London.

The business prospered and Harry chose Olney as his new location, taking on much

larger premises in Midland Road. He shrewdly perceived that by being near the train station, there would be good passing trade and better postal services, both highly important factors for the business. The business developed well and by the **1920s** Harry had the urge to expand again and selected No 56 High Street, which was a vacant piece of land after the demolition of Devon Cottage some years previously, as a perfect site for his new premises.

The Midland Road.

In **1928** local builder, George Knight, was hired to build Harry's new business premises. Harry had some grand and fanciful designs in mind - and he wanted a building the likes of which the Town had never seen before. Fortunately, George persuaded him otherwise and the more conservative building that you see today was the agreed result.

The factory was built with reclaimed materials at the time of the Great Depression and many said that it couldn't last and that the building would fall down. But the materials, although reclaimed, were of good quality and George Knight's workmanship was of the highest standards.

The only new material used on the building was for the large carvings on the front façade. Originally there were three large carvings over the front entrance - a bobbin winder, a candle stool and a bobbin stand; however, these carvings had been put up unsupported and, taking into account their location and vulnerability, they were duly moved elsewhere. One was given to a lady friend of Harry's who put it in her back garden for a number of years before it was rediscovered and

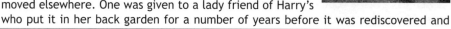

given to the Cowper and Newton Museum, where it is now on display in the Courtyard.

Despite the building being called a factory, lace was never made there. The new premises were predominately used as offices and packing rooms, although Harry did have a couple of rooms tucked away which were used for sewing lace on other articles, such as blouses, aprons, christening gowns and anything else that lent itself to lace adornment. These items were then boxed up and sold via his already booming mail order business to addresses worldwide.

Harry traded as Mrs Armstrong during his working career - he felt that women were more likely to buy lace from another woman rather than a man. He also advertised in many women's magazines and would send out calling cards to selective addresses in the Town, touting for business. In **1943**, whilst on a business trip to Scotland, Harry Armstrong died and the lace industry in Olney came to an end.

Lace making today

Lace is still made in Olney but only on a small scale and mostly as a hobby for pleasure. The Olney Lace Circle, which was formed in **1979**, is still going strong today. The group's activities include workshops, tutorials, exhibitions and demonstrations - as well as leaning to make lace, of course.

The classes and workshops are all well attended and spaces are limited but anyone interested can always contact the secretary of the Circle. Details of which can be found on the Cowper and Newton Museum Website, or directly from the Museum, who will be very happy to assist you with your enquires.

One of the many fine, pretty examples of lace made locally.

An early example of locally made shoes. Cowper and Newton Museum, Olney.

Boot and Shoe

Boot and Shoe

Evolving over the Centuries

Many years ago and until the turn of the 19th century nearly every town and village in the country had it's own shoemaker and cobbler; the shoemaker made the shoes and the cobbler repaired them.

By **1861** the National Census recorded the industry as employing 250,000 people of mixed ages and sex. This made the Boot and Shoe trade the 6th largest employment category, and one that employed more than the coal mining or the engineering industries.

Young children were employed in the trade and early references found have shown that children as young as 5 years old were working in the industry in the

A pair of child's ankle strap shoes; hand embroidered wool uppers. Amateur Olney work 1850 - 1860. Presented by Miss G Presland 1979.

13th and 14th centuries. By the age of 7 they were then taken on as apprentices and were bound to their master for the next 7 years.

In **1563**, for young children employed in the trade, the master's only obligation to his apprentices was to provide them with food and lodgings. In **1640**, after the outbreak of the Civil War, the regulations were changed and masters no longer had any obligation to provide food and lodging; it was the parent's duty to pay all of the associated costs. Despite this the children were still bound to their master and nothing was paid to them in their first year. However, in the second year they were paid 6d and this could rise to 2/6d by the time they were 7 years old.

The trade continued to grow steadily and by **1740** exploitation of the children was commonplace and stories of maltreatment and brutality were regularly heard. By **1858** the regulations for employing apprentices had changed again to take into account the Education Act. By now machines were making shoes and with education now a consideration, children could only be taken on as apprentices from the age of 12 upwards.

St Crispin: Patron Saint of Shoemakers

St Crispin is the Patron Saint of shoemakers and his feast day is the **25th October**. The latin translation for Crispin is Crispus, meaning curly, curled, wrinkled or tremulous and it was this description that was used to describe the skills the shoemakers possessed.

Boot and Shoe Process

A shoemaker's trade encompassed many skills and ranked very highly in status. Although the shoemakers worked on their own they tended to be superior craftsmen and catered for the more wealthy customers.

Once the leather had been purchased it was graded into various thicknesses. Shoes are made up of different cuts of leather, which vary in size, shape and thickness. The thinner material was used for the top of the shoe and the thicker bits were used on the soles.

The arrival of machine made shoes in the 1850s brought many benefits for everybody. These machines made the manufacturing process much, much quicker and it also produced cheaper, better-made shoes for the customer. Sales rose accordingly, which meant better wages for the workers but there was also another benefit for the wearer of the shoe. Hand made shoes did not distinguish between left and right feet and were a bit uncomfortable until they had been worn in for a while. This was taken into account and the new machines had separate lasts made for left and right feet, which gave the wearer more comfortable shoes from day one.

Who did what.....

The Clickers

It was the job of the clicker to cut the patterns out of the leather, and it was his skill and experience in being able to cut as many shoes as possible out of a piece of leather that could have an dramatic effect on the company's bank balance. It was therefore a well-paid position and one that highly ranked in the shoemaking industry.

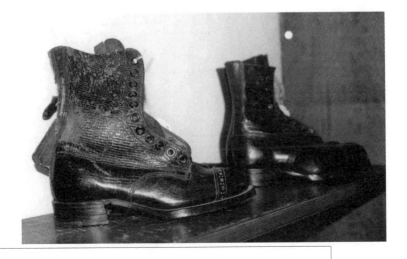

Early shoe patterns were made out of very thick card with brass beads around the edges to protect it from the sharp knives. The name " clicker " derives from the clicking noise that was heard when the knives made contact with the beads. When the clicker had cut out all he could the leftovers that remained were shaved into small pieces and used for filling the heels of the shoes- nothing was wasted!

The Binders

Once the pattern had been cut out, the leather would be passed to the binders who would sew the shoe together on a last. Because the job was not too heavy or physical, a majority of binders were women and older men. However, the machine designed to sew the heel on to the shoe required more muscle power and this task was usually given to the men.

The Finishers

The finishers or closers as they were known finished off the shoe. They also made the eyelet holes for the laces and gave the shoes a good buff and polish before putting them into a box to be sold.

Their Workshops

Some shoemakers' and cobblers' workshops are still scattered around the older parts of the Town. These small buildings might look like a coal or garden shed, even an outside toilet, but in reality it could well have been a workshop for a clicker, cobbler or closer- it's well worth a closer inspection!

Clickers Yard

Is just off Yardley Road and was the main entrance to the Cowley Shoe Factory which burnt down in **1928**.

J. W Mann 1860 – 1951

"Joseph William Mann was a major influence in the social and economic development of Olney in the latter part of the 19th century and the first half of the 20th century. A benevolent entrepreneur, with a strong social conscience and an ambition to improve the lot of his fellows, he was instrumental in changing, infinitely for the better, the lives of many of its inhabitants and he was a true father figure of modern Olney".

Gerald Mann

J.W., as he was generally known, was born in Northampton, and entered the boot and shoe trade as an apprentice clicker: the name of the person who designs shoes and cuts the patterns from which they are made.

He was an ambitious, skilled and a very productive worker who quickly became recognised as a master of his craft. In the late 1880s he came to Olney to work for William Hinde, who had a small factory in Back Street (now East Street) at the rear of 98 High Street, which is now Jeanne's Country Garden. At that time he still lived in Northampton and would walk or cycle each day, the ten miles to work and back until he found lodgings in Olney.

Hinde's workshop 98 High St, Olney.

The two men quickly built up a mutual respect for each other and in 1891 formed a partnership. The capital was valued at about £210 and comprised of machinery and stock in trade then owned by William Hinde. The partnership agreement provided that each man should draw 30 shillings per week as salary. Business flourished and very soon J.W. persuaded Hinde that they should move and open a new and much larger factory. The site chosen was at the corner of Midland Road and Wellingborough Road. The factory was extended upwards and outwards over the years and still stands today converted to private luxury apartments.

The new factory was named the Cowper Shoe Works and it was instrumental in breaking the mould of custom and practice prevailing in the boot and shoe trade in Olney, thus changing the lives and living standards of the workers employed there.

Before the advent of the Cowper Works most people engaged in the shoe trade were employed on an outworker basis. This meant that they worked from home, often in a

HINDE & MANN
Wholesale and Export Boot Manufacturers
OLNEY, BUCKS (NR NORTHAMPTON)

small shed or barn in the backyard, carrying out particular tasks in the construction of a boot or shoe: for example making heels, sewing uppers and stitching on soles. The work was mainly carried out for manufacturers in Northampton, which was the centre of the boot and shoe industry in this country, although there was one small factory in Olney; Cowley's, in Clickers Yard, which was subsequently destroyed by fire.

The pay was based on the piecework principle and quick workers could earn a reasonable income. Their outgoings were mainly payments for food, drink and rent, as very few owned their own homes. But the ability to pay for the rent and food frequently suffered because of a preoccupation with drink: a situation compounded by the extraordinary number of public houses- (in excess of 15 at the time. With the opportunity to choose between work and drink, the latter often proved more appealing!

The attraction of the new factory, a steady wage, set hours, excellent working conditions and the promise of stability, brought out-workers into regular, well-rewarded work for the first time. People now had money in their pockets and were encouraged to look to the future; the most tangible aspects of which were better living conditions and home ownership.

LODGE PLUGS

OF WELLINGBOROUGH ROAD, OLNEY.

As the local workers prosperity improved local builders such as Freeman, Fred Hart and Walter Revitt acquired the whole area that now encompasses Midland Road, Wellingborough Road, Newton Street and part of East Street for a new housing development. Employees of Hinde and Mann occupied over one hundred of these houses. Records show that a terraced house in Midland Road sold for the princely sum of £80. The financial and social benefits of this new steady employment also radiated to the many other businesses trading in Olney at that time.

The Cowper Shoe factory was commissioned into production over a period of time on an incremental basis and therefore, had been operating for well over a year before the first stage was officially opened on 12th May 1894. William Hinde and J.W. had

already established a good working relationship with their workforce and had introduced such benefits as a benevolent fund, subscribed to by the company, to support
sick staff. They also paid out an annual Christmas dividend of 7s 6d for each member
of staff. The company also organised and financed staff outings, one example of which
was a trip to Castle Ashby on 10th August 1893, when around 140 people were con-
veyed by horse-drawn brakes and carriages, for a day which included cricket, strolling
in the grounds and a visit to the house. The Olney Town Silver Band provided music.
Food was laid on and in the evening, dancing was provided to draw the day to a close.

This was typical of the benevolent attitude that Hinde and Mann adopted towards
their staff, and this was quite exceptional for a period when employers generally were
extremely autocratic and had very little regard for the welfare of their employees.
This was repaid with hard work, loyalty and quality to output, and such was the regard
for the workforce that the official opening of the Cowper Shoe Works in May 1894 was
marked by dinner and entertainment provided for by the management. The staff
reciprocated with presentations to both men.

William Hinde, in acknowledging his gift of a marble timepiece said:

" I cannot call you ladies and gentlemen, but I will call you friends. I feel entirely over-
come because it is quite an un-expected thing and I am very grateful for it. The present
and the memory will always lay dear to my heart for as long as I live for the reason
that it shows sympathy with employers. If the employers and the employed worked more
together, things would go smoother than they do in some cases. If there are grievances,
there is nothing like outspoken and straightforward dealing so that we come to agreement between ourselves. Strikes never do any good to the country. My earnest desire is
that I may be able to keep you all well employed. You might say that during the three

years that J.W. Mann and I have been together, the business has made great strides, and you will all be surprised when I tell you that in the first week we only paid £10 in wages, and last week we paid out £140".

J. W. received a handsome walnut writing desk and, after thanking the staff, he told them that when the Cowper Shoe Works first commenced production they turned out 900 pairs of footwear in the first month. In the last month the output had risen and their objective within the next few years was to achieve 9000 pairs per month. In the event the business ultimately prospered beyond his expectations. Within 15 years the high class boots and shoes which they produced were on sale in every big town in the United Kingdom, and a big export trade was developed to Germany, Austria, South Africa and India; with peak production rising to 13000 pairs of boots and shoes per week.

On the 17th June 1899 William Hinde retired and J.W. took over sole ownership of the company, but continued to trade as Hinde and Mann. He gave his former partner a gold lever English watch inscribed,

" To W. Hinde from J. W. Mann in remembrance of eight and a half years partnership".

The workforce, which had at this time risen to 330, wished him a long life and happiness and gave him an inscribed silver tea service.

The company continued to prosper for many years, concentrating on high quality footwear, but also turning over to the production of Army boots during the 1914-1918 war. For every pair of Army boots during this period he donated one halfpenny to the Northampton and General Hospital, a considerable contribution in total. During the war he worked very hard for the Red Cross and was a governor of the Hospital. He also ensured that those of his employees who were called up for war service, and their families, received comfort and help.

Like many businesses the company found things difficult in the recession period of the 1920s and 30s, and output declined against a background of low incomes and lower quality, cheaper competition. The Cowper Shoe Works was requisitioned for essential war material production in August 1940, when Lodge Plugs commenced the manufacture of spark plugs for aircraft. Lodge Plugs eventually purchased the factory and operated some time after the war, until eventually it was purchased by the Maxwell Corporation and eventually passed on to private developers for conversion into private luxury apartments.

He could clearly see the advantages not only for his own business but also for the whole of the local community.

The Family Man

When J. W. married Harriet Ann Rice they moved to Olney and lived in a house on the corner of West Street before moving to Midland Road, immediately adjacent to the factory. By this time, with a growing family (eventually three girls and three boys), he purchased No 67 and No 69 High Street at auction for £1400.

He had the premises extensively altered to a design by Northampton architect Mr. A. E. Anderson. On completion, the property was renamed Orchard House; the orchard theme was reflected in fruit, flowers and plants in the ironwork, plasterwork, leaded windows, interior woodwork, furniture and many art nouveau features. Orchard House was the first house in Olney to be lit by electricity. There was a purpose-built engine house in the garden, which housed a 3-cylinder Austin generator, driven by a petrol engine, which could be started from the house to provide a 50-volt supply of electricity. This system powered the house until J.W.'s death in 1951; and a modified version is still in use today.

The house had a large billiards' room and this was useful for both social and business purposes. J.W. would combine both. On one occasion, around 1904, when there was a battalion of Lancers stationed at Weston Underwood for exercises, J. W. invited the Colonel-in-Charge for a game

Mr and Mrs JW Mann.

of billiards with C.M. Allen and other local businessmen. They had a convivial evening, accompanied by a few whiskeys and cigars, by the end of which J.W. Mann had obtained an order for boots for the whole battalion.

Not only was J.W. an astute businessman, he was also a meticulous dresser. He was a familiar sight walking down Olney High Street in the mornings, lunchtimes and evenings dressed in his bowler hat, silver topped cane and grey spats over his Hinde and Mann shoes.

In the winter months of 1908 to 1910 J. W presented all the poorly shod children at the local school with new boots. Boots were the standard footwear for children in those days and many children benefited from his kindness. His paternal regard for his staff was to the fore again on Coronation day, 17th June 1911, when he presented gifts to all of his staff. Men over 21 years received 10/-, those aged 17 years to 21 years received 5/- and girls and boys under the age of 17 received 2/6d.

After the First World War there was a debate in the town as to a suitable memorial for the fallen. Some wanted a War Memorial whilst others thought funds raised should go towards the Town Hall. J.W. was strongly in favour of the stone memorial that we have today and donated one hundred guineas towards the cost, ensuring its erection.

J.W. was largely instrumental in bringing the telephone service to the Town. The local press announced in January 1913, that with the assistance of J.W. Mann, Chairman of the Parish Council and the largest employer of labour in the town, " Olney is to be given a continuous telephonic service. This will be a great benefit to tradesmen and businessmen in the town and we are naturally very grateful for the interest Mr. Mann has taken in bringing about this so desirable innovation".

J. W. was involved with many organisations on a voluntary basis both in Olney and the surrounding areas. The list below is a small sample of what he was actively involved with.

Chairman, Olney Parish Council
Rural District Councillor, 1913 - 1937 – Newport Pagnell
Member of the Olney Feoffee Charity
Member of the Fire Brigade Committee
President of the Olney Cricket Club
President of the Olney Bowls Club
President of the Olney Football Club
Justice of the Peace in 1906
Freemason
Member for the Liberal 200 Club
Member of the Congregational Chapel

Whilst he chaired many committees, the one committee that he loathed, but considered to be his duty to serve, was the Assessment Committee that operated during the 1920s and 1930s to decide individual applications from the unemployed for relief (financial help). He said of all the public offices he found this one the most distressing and, for a period of time, he paid some of the Olney people out of his own pocket to carry out work in the development of the recreation ground. As a Rural District Councillor he also ensured that Olney was one of the first areas to benefit from main drainage. As a result of his initiatives, the council estate on Moores Hill was built, a modern development for its time.

In the 1930s the Olney Fire Brigade, then owned by the Parish Council, was in a perilous state. The equipment was worn out and there was no money to replace it. Alec Crouch a Rural District Councillor and J.W. worked together to persuade the Rural District Council to accept full financial responsibility for the Fire Brigade, although it was manned by volunteers. At the outbreak of war the local brigade became part of the National Fire Service and eventually became the responsibility of the Bucks County Council. During this period, and to the current day, local people are still manning it.

J. W's wife Harriett died in 1926 age 69 years, but he continued to live in Orchard House until his death in 1951 aged 91 years. The house was then acquired by Bob Soul who has lovingly retained all the original features that made it so unique.

The impact and influence of J W Mann was encapsulated in a very moving appreciation penned by his former employee Alec Crouch. (Extract from which appears below) who whilst at variation with J W's politics also shared a strong common interest in the welfare of their fellows and local community generally.

An Appreciation from Alec Crouch

"With the death of Joseph William Mann a period of progress in Olney of which he was the chief architect has come to an end.

In its turbulent history many men have by their wit, eloquence and plausibility shone for a time in its social and economic life, most of them left little of enduring worth behind them, sometimes a scar remained, some times a faint memory of their passing lingered, but J W Mann was different, his outlook on life was not one of self-aggrandisement, nor had he an urge for social climbing, he had a passionate desire to produce something worthwhile, something which would raise the wages and better the conditions of the people around him, and in this he succeeded.

At the time of which I write, Olney consisted of the High Street from the river bridge to the "Queen" public house, East Street and West Street, a few houses in Weston Road and what in an earlier age the poet Cowper had described as, the abyss of Silver End.

Leading off the High Street were four farm yards and a number of alleys or courts which connected with the streets on either side, in these courts were scores of two-roomed dwellings crowded with a mass of humanity hopelessly in debt from one years end to another, the conditions under which they lived were aptly described by a doggerel of the period which ran, and every Monday morning, shortly after eight, there's a row in Flood's Court about Flood's rent.

Most people worked in the shoe trade, but owing to frequent bankruptcy and other causes, work was intermittent and their poverty was appalling by modern standards.
Such was the position when J W Mann came to Olney from Northampton, he was a master of his craft, so skilled and speedy that his output equalled that of a man and a half. I remember him starting in business with the late Mr W Hinde, the first man he employed is still living in Olney, and I was his errand boy.

From the first day the progress of the firm was phenomenal and spectacular, within fifteen years the high class boots and shoes they produced were on sale in

every big town and city in the United Kingdom.
After about ten years the partnership was dissolved and Mr Mann went on to develop a big export trade to Germany, Austria, South Africa and India, his peak production rising to thirteen thousand pairs of boots and shoes weekly. During this period what was known as Station Estate was developed. On one side of Dartmouth Road, part of East Street, the whole of Newton Street, Cowper Street,

JW's Daimler at Olney Station collecting the Marquis of Northampton and his wife for the Alexander Rose Day Celebrations.

Midland Road and Wellingborough Road were built. It shows the prosperity the firm had brought to Olney when it is realised that of those houses at least a hundred were owned by people in his employ.

As chairman of the Parish Council, and a member of the Rural District Council, he put through a drainage scheme which has been an untold blessing. In 1922, mainly by his initiative, the Council estate at Moores Hill was built and is today one of the most pleasing lay-outs in the district.
Olney today is prosperous, it has its Tannery, Lodge Plugs and furniture factory. It owns twenty acres of recreation ground, sixty acres of allotments, bathing place and has money invested in the funds. Its courts have been closed, the abyss of Silver- end has been purged, it is a transformation of which any man might be proud and in the main it is due to the energy and skill of Joseph William Mann. I do not mourn his passing, his years were many, his work ably done, but I count it a pleasure to have been permitted to associate with one capable of doing so much to lighten the burden of his fellow men".
There can be no better tribute to the life and achievements of J W Mann than this".

The Olney Tannery

In the late 1700s as you approached Olney from Emberton you would have seen Olney's Tannery on your left hand side. It was a large development that stood close to the river's edge and at that time the Wagstaff family owned both the Tannery and Bridge House.

It is unknown if there was an earlier "Tan Yard" than this date in Olney but the first mention of one can be found in a letter from William Cowper to his friend the Rev John Newton. The letter describes how one of Cowper's beloved pet hares had escaped from Orchard Side and was rescued from one of the Tannery's lime pits.

"She pushed for the town again, and soon after she entered it sought shelter in Mr Wagstaff's tan yard, adjoining to old Mr Drake Sturges. Harvestmen were at supper and saw her from the opposite way. There she encountered the tar pits full of water, and whilst she was struggling from one pit, and plunging into another, and almost drowned, one of the men drew her out by her ears and secured her. She was then well washed in a bucket, to get the lime out of her coat, and brought back home in a sack at ten o'clock".

In 1798 the Posse Cometatus of Olney, which listed the occupations and trades of men between the ages of 16-60, listed William Wagstaff as a gentleman, and his sons, John and Thomas as tanners. The family continued living at Bridge House until 1840, when the Tannery and the house were then sold to Joseph Palmer.

Joseph Palmer moved into Bridge House with his wife and five children and went on to develop the Tannery into a flourishing business, and one that earned him a good reputation throughout England. Much later the business was allowed to lapse, the vats were later demolished and timber was sold for firewood- the Tannery looked a very sorry site.

On the 5th February 1894, after a lengthy illness, Joseph Palmer died at the grand old age of 93. His funeral took place in Olney on the 10th February and his body was buried in the family vault in the presence of many mourners and watchers. Four years later the Tannery and Bridge House were put up for sale at public auction and on the 16th June 1898 William Edward Pebody, a Chrome Tanner from Northampton, pur-chased the properties.

William E Pebody founded his business in 1878 at Lower Mounts, Northampton. In 1896 his brother Joseph had joined him and the company became W.E & J. Pebody Ltd., Chrome Tanners, Northampton. William, who was a recent widower, decided to move into Bridge House with his seven children, (4 daughters, 3 sons) and continued to work with his brother Joseph on a new process, chrome tanning. This was a process that had been invented in both France and America but was still in its experimental stages in England. William and Joseph spent many long hard hours trying to perfect the process for their business and eventually their perseverance paid off. Pebody's became one of the first companies in England to adopt the process and produce this type of leather.

Boot and Shoe

In 1902 William married Emma Brock and with the new process working well he remained in Olney to oversee production whilst Joseph undertook the selling.

In **1914** war broke out and there was strong demand for good quality leather that could withstand the trenches. Chrome leather was found to be ideal and the Tannery soon became very busy. To cope with this increased demand some of the existing buildings were expanded and a new large three-storied building was constructed. (This building caught fire in **1944** and was later rebuilt but on a much larger scale). At the height of the 1st World War a 360-horse power Petrie steam engine was purchased from a Lancashire Mill and the business continued to do well but, like so many others, suffered somewhat during the Great Depression.

In **1934**, gaining from the changes made by the Government concerning exporting and importing of leather, the Tannery became active again and in 1938, in order to provide the factory with a more constant supply of quality water, a series of shallow wells were installed at Goosey Bridge, Weston Road.
Just before William died he sold the company's site at Northampton to the Anglian Building Society who intended to make it their headquarters, but in 1939 war broke out and they never moved in. Instead they let the Pebody family carry on using the building until **1961**, when the remainder of the administration staff was finally moved to Olney.

By the **1950s** the leather market had become competitive again but after William's death the Tannery lost some impetus and a number of key personnel left. To engender some fresh life into the business, a new manager was appointed in **1952** and he introduced a new tanning process, Aniline leather. This process was successful for a number of years but it created a problem with the effluent, which needed to be disposed of simply and safely. Much time and money was given to resolving this difficulty and eventually, in 1978, having spent something like £250,000 on the project, a large plant was installed which produced a satisfactory conclusion.

Since William first purchased the Tannery in **1898** there have been four generations of the Pebody family working in the business and during their time they have produced high quality leather, which was exported all around the world.
In 1998 the leather production was transferred to Northampton and in March **1999** production in Olney ceased; just six months short of Pebody's 100th anniversary in the Town.
The land has since been sold to Bloor Homes, who are now developing the site into a new housing area for Olney.

An early view of Weston Underwood.

Weston Underwood

Weston Underwood

By Mark Covington

Situated two miles south of Olney is Weston Underwood, formerly a hamlet belonging to Olney. There are many reasons why Weston Underwood is so very interesting. It is a deceptively sleepy looking village in which houses are rarely seen for sale. The local community is well-grounded, long established and extremely protective of their village and, as you read on, you will understand why.

Weston Underwood High street c, 1900.

The strong links and traditions that Olney now has and what we now take for granted, such as the Olney Coat of Arms, originate from Weston Underwood. The Coat of Arms or the Town Crest was found many years ago on a brass grave plate belonging to Elizabeth, wife of Sir Walter Hungerford and later the wife of Robert Throckmorton. The crest, which represents both families, was adopted for general use by Olney Town Council until **1977**. In the year of the Silver Jubilee, Olney Town Council encouraged local artists within the area to recreate and update the Crest.

Sir John Throckmorton.

A design submitted by C. R Perkins was selected and approved as the new Town Crest and was later incorporated into the medallion of the Mayor of Olney's chain of office.

Weston Underwood is also abundantly full of interesting features connected with William Cowper, poet, translator of Homer and one of England's great letter writers. Cowper moved from Olney to Weston Underwood in November **1786** as a resident guest of the Throckmorton family, and stayed with them until a few years before his death. The house is now known as Cowper's Lodge and is situated along the High Street.

Back in the 1400s floods often made the roads in and around Olney impassable for many weeks, sometimes months. This caused problems for local people: one being how to bury their dead as all burials were carried out in Olney, as there was no church at Weston Underwood at the time. And so an application was made to the Pope to make Weston Underwood an Independent Parish and to provide the townsfolk with their own church. This was quickly granted and ever since, Weston Underwood has been on its own and has had no problems with burials.

In **1381**, John de Olney purchased land at Weston Underwood and records show that he had his own private chapel in his home at the Old Mansion, which was later demolished in **1827**. All that remains of the house today are the Clock House, Weston House, The Chapel and the Laundry Cottage, all of which are now privately owned residences. John de Olney died in **1405** and is buried in the churchyard at Weston Underwood.

In **1446** the Weston Underwood Estate passed into the hands of the Throckmorton family. As you enter the village through the stone pillars, known locally as the Knobs, they bear a strong and silent reminder of the family and their existence. They also give us an indication of just how grand and prestigious the estate once was, even the Knobs at one time had their own gates, which were manned and locked at night.

An Amusing Tale...

Did you know that the Knobs have surprisingly only ever had 2 known tangles with motor vehicles? In **1970** they were widened to their current size and considering how long they have been there, and the heavy traffic Weston Underwood now has to cope with, they have survived very well.

On one occasion a nameless farmer / butcher was on his way back home from Olney, having just indulged in several pints of the local ale, when his vehicle hit one of the stone pillars and sent one of the tops flying off! Fortunately, it wasn't a complete disaster; the top didn't break, which probably had something to do with the soft padding that was in the back of the farmer's pick-up van at the time. The top was later duly replaced and has remained there ever since.

The Throckmorton Family

The Throckmorton family spared no expense in creating wonderful gardens and park areas in Weston Underwood, many of which caught William Cowper's attention and are mentioned in several of his works. Some of the areas of interest today are now on privately owned land and not open to the visiting public. So I have taken the opportunity, and with the current owner's permission, of updating the existing pictures of these items with never before seen engravings of the areas, alongside long overdue photographs of what they look like today; a real mixture of the old and new combining forces and giving you the best of both worlds.

The Rustic Bridge

John Higgins built the rustic bridge in 1740 at the request of Sir. Robert Throckmorton. The bridge spanned a deep brook that meandered through the park, and is still standing today.

The Alcove

The alcove was built in 1750, again by Mr John Higgins, for the Throckmorton Estate. The Alcove was originally at the end of a lime tree avenue and could be reached from the Rustic Bridge along the northern boundary of the park. The Throckmorton family lost interest in the Alcove on account of a terrible accident that befell the place some twenty years after it was built. Mr Higgins' son was carrying out essential repairs and re-painting the roof when he lost his footing and fell to his death. Ever since, the family considered it to be a place of ill fortune and out of respect to the Higgins family they never returned to it. Sadly, and despite much public protest, the lime trees were felled in 1928.

The Gothic Temple

Built for the Throckmorton Estate the Gothic Temple is still standing today, albeit in the now closed Bird Gardens. The Gothic Temple is of a similar design to, and should not be confused, with the Alcove.

In front of the Temple is a hexagonal platform, which was surrounded by evergreens, shrubs and elms. In the centre of the Temple was a majestic acacia and at the end of the vista once stood a bust of Homer, which is understood to have been in the possession of William Cowper when he resided at the Lodge.

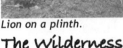

Lion on a plinth.

Fop's Urn.

The Wilderness

From the avenue of limes, which has since disappeared, you would have entered the Wilderness via an elegant iron gate, which was constructed in Chinese style. On your left hand side, and at the end of a grassy walk, was a finely carved statue of a lion on a plinth. Yews and elms mingle with the drooping foliage of the laburnum tree; this forms a border and has a handsome urn on each side. On the base of one of the urns is an engraved epitaph to Neptune, Sir John Throckmorton's dog. On the base of the other is an epitaph dedicated to another dog, Fop, Lady Throckmorton's spaniel.

These urns and the lion are still about today and in a reasonable condition, albeit a bit green looking.

The Spinney or the Shrubbery

No longer standing today the entrance was via a gate on the left hand side of the road as you approached Olney from Weston Underwood. A stately sycamore, a spreading oak, fir, beech and elms made this a beautiful and tranquil spot. It was here, secluded from view that the Moss House with its lowly thatched roof once stood. William Cowper visited this part of the park on many occasions and admired it so much that he had a board put up which read:

"Here, free from riot's hated noise
Be mine, ye calmer, purer joy
A book or a friend bestows;
Far from the storms that shake the great,
Contentment's gale shall fan my seat,
And sweeten my repose".

This board though was stolen but it was promptly replaced with another – with the following lines being taken from the 6th book of the Task:

"No noise is here, or none that hinders thought.
Stillness, accompanied with sounds so soft,
Charms more than silence. Mediation here
May think down hours to moments. Here the heart
May give a useful lesson to the head,
And learning wiser grow without his books".

Cowper's Oak

Alas no longer there today, this tree, with a girth of 22 feet and 6 inches, once stood on a beautiful spot and even inspired William Cowper to write about it. The following notice was displayed on this magnificent oak -

"Out of respect for the memory of William Cowper, the Marquis of Northampton is particularly desirous of preserving this Oak. Notice is hereby given that any person defacing or otherwise injuring will be prosecuted according to the Law".

The tree sadly burnt down in 1950.

Village life today

Village life is never dull, although perhaps a little slow and sleepy which is only to be expected with a village of this size. It didn't enter the world of technology until the late **1940s**, when delivery was taken of the red telephone kiosk, which now stands outside the Post Office. The telephone line was a party line shared with the Post Office; the phone in the Post Office rang twice before the kiosk phone rang! In those days the village bobby on his pushbike had to wait at the phone box for a call from his headquarters.

On the **4th December 1894**, the Parish Council was formed and meetings were held in the local school. Mr Thomas Dart was chosen as chairman and the following were nominated as members -

Mr Charles Adams: Gardener
Mr Alfred Fisher: Shoemaker
Mr William Higgins: Farmer
Mr Stephen William Stewart: Farmer
Mr Frederick George Stokes: Priest

The Post Office at Weston Underwood.

In the early years the Council only seemed to meet once a year. The main purpose was to discuss the amounts in the Parish Charities - Dudley, Feoffee, Spinks, and Maids Meadow, which today are collectively known as the Weston Underwood Charities. Ancestors of more well known village family names of Stewart, Covington and Graves all appear as members of the Parish Council in the early years. In the early **1950s** Stan Clarke and Mr. Fred Foster both became members of the Council.

The village today only has one Public House and a Post Office; long gone is the village shop and Charlie Covington's Blacksmiths and Forge that once stood at the end of the High Street. But most of the villagers who live there now are happy enough with what they have and are content with the quiet village way of life. However, this all changes when there's an event to be celebrated; they then stand united, dust off the flags, make the effort and put on a really good show!
Here are a couple of the more memorable celebration days that Weston Underwood has put on.

Wings and Wheels – 22nd June 1991

The Wheels: a varied display and demonstration of all types of motor vehicles, from Land Rovers to the Rolls Royce Silver Ghost, the most valuable car in the world.

The Wings: micro-lights, helicopters and even a fly past from the Royal Air Force Battle of Britain Memorial Flight.

A truly superb day and I am sure one that will be remembered by many for a very long time.

The Queen's Golden Jubilee Celebrations – Tuesday 4th June 2002

A well-supported day that was held on the village green and even the weather behaved itself. There was a fancy dress competition for the children, a bouncy castle and afternoon tea was served in the true picnic style that many of us grew up with in the past. The adults joined in with the tug-of-war, and were cooled down by the bar, which was on hand to dispense refreshing quenchers for the hard earned thirsts! A hog roast and a barn dance saw the evening to a finish and everybody had a jolly good time!

St Peter and St Paul Parish Church Olney.

Olney's Parish Church

Pilgrimages

There is an island there is no going
to but in a small boat the way
the saints went, travelling the gallery
of frightened faces of
the long-drowned, munching the gravel
of its beaches. So I have gone
up the salt lane to the building
with the stone altar and the candles
gone out, and kneeled and lifted
my eyes to the furious gargoyle
of the owl that is like a god
gone small and resentful. There
is no body in the stained window
of the sky now. Am I too late?
Were they too late also, those
first pilgrims? He is such a fast
God, always before us and
leaving as we arrive.
There are those here
not given to prayer, whose office
is the blank sea that they say daily.
What they listen to is not
hymns but the slow chemistry of the soil
that turns saints' bones to dust,
dust to an irritant of the nostril.

There is no time on this island.
The swinging pendulum of the tide
has no clock; the events
are dateless. These people are not
late or soon; they are just
here with only the one question
to ask? which life answers
by being in them. Is it I
who ask. Was the pilgrimage
I made to come to my own
self, to learn that in times
like these and for one like me
God will never be plain and
out there, but dark rather and
inexplicable, as though he were in here?

R. S Thomas.

Olney's Parish Church

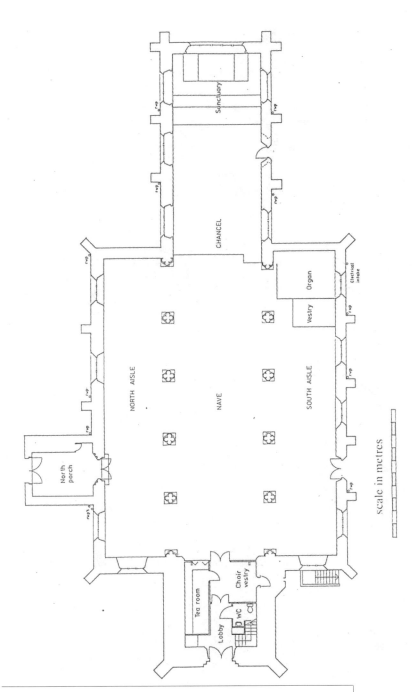

ST. PETER AND ST. PAUL, OLNEY

Sanctuary

CHANCEL

Organ

Vestry

Electrical
intake

NORTH AISLE

NAVE

SOUTH AISLE

North
porch

scale in metres

Tea room

Choir
vestry

Lobby

WC

Cd

Olney Parish Church

"Olney's Parish Church has much to offer; from the moment you walk through the front gates you are walking in the ancient footsteps of famous and notable people who have made a very valuable contribution to local history".

St Peter and St Paul's

It is situated at the southern end of the Olney and is without the shadow of a doubt the oldest surviving building left in the Town. An earlier church (albeit a much smaller one) was thought to have existed at the northern end of the Town roughly where the Castle pub now stands.

This charming 13th century Church of St Peter and St Paul's is one of Olney's finest jewels, not only is it a magnificent structure in its design and build, it's also packed with fascinating historical information. Today, like many Churches throughout England, Olney's Church is self-funded and heavily relies on its congregation for its support and continuity. The running costs today exceed well over a £1,000 per week, all of which are covered by public donations and various fund-raising events, which are held in the Town throughout the year.

St Peter and St Paul: The Saints

St Peter was a fisherman by trade, trained by his father, and he was Jesus' first Apostle and the first Pope.

St Paul was a Jew and initially an unremitting persecutor of Christians until experiencing an awe-inspiring conversion to Christianity, being struck blind temporarily, whilst travelling on a journey to Damascus. After his conversion to Christianity he regained his sight and thereafter became the foremost preacher of the faith.

Both St Peter and St Paul were martyred for their faith and their feast day is celebrated on the 29th June, the same day as the Church holds its Cherry Fair. Both saints are the patron saints of the boot and shoe trade in Olney, predominantly the main trade in the Town many years ago.

Sir Nikolaus Pevsner

After a visit to Olney in the **1950s**, Sir Nikolaus Pevsner, a noted and respected Art and Architectural historian, made the following reference to the Church in his **1960s** book entitled "Buckinghamshire", one of a series he wrote on "The Buildings of England",

THE PARISH CHURCH, OLNEY

"St Peter and St Paul's church is unmistakable with its tall C14 spire. The tower is tall too. It has diagonal buttresses. On its top the spire starts with very short broaches, hardly noticeable as tall pinnacles stand on them. The spire has four sets of lucarnes, all in the cardinal directions. The early C14 is the period which prevails in the church. Very tall three-light windows with flowing tracery. In the chancel the five-light East window is over-restored. The Chancel NW and SW windows are of the low-side type and have transoms. Inside, against the North wall is the Easter Sepulchre. The tomb-chest has quatrefoil panels in a very crisply and richly ornamented framework. Large and airy interior, with Five-bay arcades with quatrefoil piers and arches with two sunk quadrants. Chancel arch with three sunk quadrants dying into the imposts. Tower arch is triple-chamfered, also dying. It is a pity that the church has no clerestory. The segmentally vaulted plaster ceiling lies somewhat low on the nave".

Glossary of Ecclesiastical Terms

Arcade	A series of arches supported by piers or columns.
Aumbry	A recess or cupboard used to hold consecrated elements.
Chancel	The eastern area of the church where the choir and ministers sit.
Lucarne	A small window in the Spire.
Nave	Main body of the church.
Piscina	A basin for washing Communion or Mass vessels.
Quatrefoil	Four lobes formed by a circular shape.
Reredos	A painted or carved screen used as decoration at the back of the altar.
Sanctuary	A part of the church where the altar is situated.
Sedilia	A seat for priests, usually found in threes Olney has four!
Tracery	Intersecting rib work in the upper part of the window.
Sepulchre	A burial vault, tomb or grave or an Easter Sepulchre, an alcove in some churches where Eucharistic elements are kept from Good Friday to Easter.

A Tour around the Church

The Entrance

The stone columns and gate at the main entrance of the Church were originally from The Great House that stood nearby. When the Great House was demolished in **1833** the builders clearing the site decided to make good use of these historical items and placed them where they stand today.

The Roof

As you look at the roofing of the Church you will notice the different pitches. In **1807** major building work was carried out as a large fracture had appeared in the north wall. The weight of the old roof, which was lead and wood, had begun to push down on the internal arcades and was the cause of the problem. So the old roof was dismantled and a new one was constructed, but this time 6-8 feet lower that the original. The lead from the old roof was sold to a Birmingham dealer and the beautiful wooden beams were auctioned off in the churchyard.

The Spire

The spire is just one of the many fine features of the Church and, standing at just a little over 185 feet and host to 16 windows, it blends in beautifully with the surrounding landscape and can be seen from many miles away.

There are two things that strike you about the spire, the first being the bulge that it appears to have. It is easy to think that this bulge is a trick of the light but apparently this entasis, as it is correctly known, is meant to be there. When the spire was erected the sides were built on a slightly convex angle in order to achieve the effect of straightness. If this had not been taken into account during the course of building, the spire could have ended up bent like a banana.

The second is the tip of the spire; the stonework is two different shades. During a bad storm in 1884 the spire was struck by lightning and had to be re-built later that year. The original stonework is 500 years older than that of the replacement, hence the different colour, but in a few more hundred years (God willing that there will be no more lightning strikes) the spire should have blended back into a single shade.

The Weathercock

Whilst the repairs to the tip of the spire were being carried out the opportunity was taken to clean and re-guild the weathercock.

The weathercock's vital statistics:

Height:	2ft
Length:	2ft 9" from tip to beak
Other Information:	Several bullet holes through the tail, either from past civil wars or locals. There are also several inscriptions.

Main Inscription:	*"I never crow, but stand to show, whence winds do blow, 1829".*
Additional Inscription:	H Gauntlett (Vicar, 1829) B.C: Benjamin Coles, Churchwarden W.L: William Lord, Churchwarden J.H: John Herring, Churchwarden
1884 Inscription:	J. P. Langley (Vicar) John Garrard, Churchwarden Thos. T. Cole, Churchwarden

The Bells

Bell	Diameter	Strike Note	Weight Approx	Date	Founder	Comments
Tenor	4' - 4"	288	24-3-14	1682	Henry Bagley, Chacombe	The biggest bell. Inscribed "God save the King" There are also 9 Charles 2nd shillings cast in it.
7th	3' - 10"	325	17-3-11	1733	Thomas Russell, Wootton	
6th	3' - 8"	361	14-3-21	1631	Robert Atton, Buckingham	Inscribed "Robert Atton made me".
5th	3' - 3"	385	10-3-17	1699	Henry Bagley, Ecton	Inscribed "Robert Bagley made me".
4th	2' - 11"	433	7-2-23	1599	Newcombe & Watts, Bedford	The oldest bell.
3rd	2' - 10"	481	8-0-22	1682	Henry Bagley I, Chacombe	
2nd	2' - 9"	542	7-0-13	1912	Alfred Bowell, Ipswich	
Treble	2' - 8"	582	7-0-23	1912	Alfred Bowell, Ipswich	

Wild Life in the Spire

The churchyard is host to many kinds of creatures but Pippistrelle bats, birds and owls are particularly drawn to the spire and it's one of the reasons why the windows have been netted. Wildlife in public areas does need to be controlled and these birds could make a real mess and cause untold chaos if they should get inside.

The Gargoyles

Many of the Gargoyles date back to the 14th century but some of them have been repaired and restored during this time. These cheeky little fellows are scattered about both inside and outside the Church and, despite surviving the ravages of time, they are all in pretty good shape. They are all beautiful (when you consider their great age), uniquely different and it's great fun finding the one who owns either the ugliest or funniest face; you're rather spoilt for choice – that's if your neck can take the strain!

The Clock

Messrs. Lesson of Birmingham installed the Church clock in 1887 to commemorate Queen Victoria's Jubilee. It cost £280 of which Lord Dartmouth donated £100. The Westminster chimes that you hear when the clock strikes were added in 1903.

The Bell Tower

The tower is home to 8 bells, the oldest of which dates back to 1599 and was made by Newcombe & Watts from Bedford. The bell frame has been re-built and re-treated over the years but some parts of the frame date back well over 300 years earlier.

The North Porch

The north porch was re-built - and the earlier porch of 1686 extended - in 1807 as part of major repairs to the Church. At the same time an extra room was added over the porch, which was later used as a schoolroom.

Perhaps this is now the time to tell you about the Imp before you enter the Church for a good look around.

The Little Imp

The little imp is a small reminder of when the Parish of Olney belonged to the Diocese of Lincoln. He's a cute little fellow and children of all ages really enjoy looking for

him inside the Church. I'm not going to spoil your fun and tell you where he is, but will give you a clue:

" I'm on a wall low down,

just resting taking a pew,

with the bald headed vicar as my main view".

A Look around the Inside

As you enter the front doors of the Church you immediately feel the airiness and calm that this haven has to offer. While wandering past the two arcades with 5 bays and separate south and north aisles, you see the massive main window - you can hardly miss it - it's

beautiful and it immediately catches your attention.

Records show that there were no fixed seats in Olney church until the early part of the 15th century and with an ever-increasing congregation it necessitated more space being added. In 1723 Mathew Maryot, clerk and sexton of the church, installed a public gallery at his own expense; and in 1765 another gallery was also added to meet the demand of the day- but both of these were later removed and never replaced.

The Windows

The Church has numerous stained glass windows all of which are truly beautiful, ornately designed, very old and absorbingly interesting. Each one depicts a special story and powerful message.

As you enter through the north porch doors the first window on your left is a local window that depicts past notable influences of Olney and was erected shortly after the First World War in thanksgiving for those who returned home. It immortalises the memory of and the contribution made to the Town by the following people. A map outlining more in-depth information about the window can be found close by.

Other influences in the windows...

The Rev. John Newton Influence

John Newton, former slave trader and curate of the Parish, is aptly depicted with his slaves. There is also an open book, the Olney Hymn book in which the Rev John Newton wrote "Amazing Grace", which can be seen on the open page of the book.

The William Cowper Influence

Depicted in the window is the great man himself along with his home, Orchard Rise (now the Museum) and his three hares, Tiny, Bess and Puss.

Then we have his tree, The Great Oak at Yardley Chase, from which he drew great inspiration and often visited.

Other Local Influences

The praying, kneeling figure is Dr Henry Gauntlet, the father of English Church Music. In his youth he spent many years as an organist of the Church and later went on to write well over a 1,000 hymns during his life including "Once in Royal David's City".

The Book of Remembrance

Adorning the sides of local window, in the north porch, are the banners from The Royal British Legion and underneath them is the Book of Remembrance. For More information about the Book of Remembrance see Today's Events.

The Pulpits

There are two pulpits in the Church and the one most currently used stands at the east end of the nave and was built by local builders in **1883**. The other, which is no longer used, is the John Newton pulpit, which

stands nicely preserved in a corner of the Church having a well-earned rest from its busy past. John Newton's coffin plate dated **1807** also hangs on the wall next to his pulpit.

The Fonts

There are also two fonts in the church and again, like the pulpits,

The Pulpit used today.

only one of them is currently used. (So babies are no longer baptised at both ends!!) The oldest font, which is no longer used, dates back to the early part of the 16th century and stands close to the main doors of the Church. However, it does still sit on its original castors and could, despite its age and great weight, be moved around should the need ever arise. The font used today was presented to the Church in **1897**, by the Rev J. P Langley, in commemoration of Queen Victoria's Diamond Jubilee.

The John Newton Pulpit.

The Organ

Built by Binns of Leeds at a cost of £594, the organ was regarded by the manufacturers as being their finest piece to date, and was proudly installed in the Church in **1907**.

The Sanctuary

The Easter Sepulchre

Set in the north wall of the Sanctuary (on your left) is the Easter Sepulchre, which dates back to the 14th century and is ornately designed with quatrefoils in a decorative frame.

The Aumbry

Just a little distance from the Easter Sepulchre and tucked away in the corner of the Church is the Aumbry. This sacred tabernacle contains the reserved Sacrament, kept available for the giving of Communion to the sick and housebound.

The Reredos

This stunning screen that was built by Jones & Willis of London is made from Caen stone with pillars of black, grey and red Devonshire marble. The attention to detail is amazing; the reredos depicts the pastoral lamb with side panels emblematic of the four evangelists. The top panels are diapered and filled with crocketed labels, the elaborately carved tracery is in the Gothic style and has figureheads at the top of the pillars with four pinnacles surmounting the centre.

The reredos was erected in memory of John William Garrard in **1896** and has recently been lovingly and carefully preserved which, I am pleased to say, has further enhanced its magnificent beauty.

The ancient **Piscina** can be seen on the east wall in the north aisle.

The Sedilia

On the opposite wall to the Easter Sepulchre is another beautiful feature of the Church, the Sedilia. Ministers use this recently restored seat during services; usually there are only three seats in a Sedilia but Olney is blessed with four.

The Angels

If you look up towards the chancel's roof you will notice the eight winged guardians beaming straight back down at you. They were erected in 1807, when the major repairs were being carried out, and re-painted in the late 1940s. The angels are beautiful pieces of ecclesiastical art, they are all different and are a sheer pleasure to look at and admire.

Did you Know...... Worship

On the 30th March 1851 an ecclesiastical census was carried out throughout England with the intention and purpose of recording attendance levels in places of worship. This is what was printed about Olney and recorded in the Buckinghamshire Record Society, Vol.27

Morning General Congregation	320
Morning Sunday Scholars	210
Morning Total	530
Afternoon General Congregation	350
Afternoon Sunday Scholars	225
Afternoon Total	575
Evening General Congregation	350
Evening Sunday Scholars	80
Evening Total	430

The Churchyard

Fauna

The wildlife in Olney's churchyard is carefully controlled and managed to a reasonable and sustainable level. The roof ledges make ideal nesting areas for sparrows, house martins and swifts, whilst the spire makes an excellent viewing spot for potential prey for the kestrels and owls that visit frequently. Even the compost heap is a busy place and provides much needed food and shelter for the hedgehogs, slowworms and mice.

Flora

There are in total over 100 different species of wildflowers in the churchyard, as well as nearly 90 different species of lichen. The grass in some areas is left long and uncut purposely; not only does it encourage the wild flowers to grow, it also allows them to spread their seeds in the way that nature intended.

Other areas of interest

The Oldest Grave

Unfortunately, some one has to be first and every churchyard does have one. Olney's oldest grave, made from local limestone and dating back to 1667, in the reign of Charles 2nd, is inscribed "Robert Sharp, died 23rd December 1667".

Memorials

There are 637 memorials in the churchyard and many of them are poignant reminders of Olney's past. Some of the more elaborate monuments include a war grave from the 2nd World War and the Hipwell Angel, whose memorial is dedicated to a family member of the Hipwell family, the Town's one-time local brewers.

As most of the graves are very old in this part of the churchyard, many of the inscriptions are now badly weathered but if you are looking for someone or a particular stone, don't worry, help is at hand.

Inside, at the rear of the Church, is the churchwarden's chest, on top of which is a green book. This book contains a record of all the graves in the immediate churchyard - but not in the cemetery over the road. Most required information is to be found in this book but it may not be removed from the Church. If there are still problems in tracing someone, the rectory might be able to assist and the phone number is on the notice board in the churchyard.

The John Newton Tomb

John Newton was a former slave trader and curate of the Parish in Olney. In his later years he moved as Vicar to the parish of St Mary, Woolnoth in the City of London, where he continued to preach and

expound his faith. It was here he spent his final days and was ultimately buried in the churchyard by the side of his wife.

Some years later, London Underground were carrying out essential building works to the line and the Rev John Newton's tomb – and that of his wife Mary – needed to be excavated and moved so that the works could be carried out. So they made their final journey back to Olney, where Mary's father, George Catlett, is buried and they were laid to rest close to where the Great House once stood, a building which played an important part in John Newton's life.

John Newton and his wife were re-interred in Olney on the very cold and bitter morning of **January 25th 1893**. His tomb is made of Cornish granite and the top has been cut from one piece. It weighs 28 hundredweight and takes at least 28 fit and strapping young men to lift it.

The Inscription on his tomb reads

"John Newton, Clerk, once an infidel and libertine, a servant of slaves in Africa was by the rich mercy of our Lord and Saviour Jesus Christ preserved, restored, pardoned and appointed to preach the faith he has long laboured to destroy, nearly 16 years as curate of this parish and, 28 years as rector of St. Mary, Woolnoth.

These remains were removed from the church of St. Mary, Woolnoth, in the city of London, and re-interred here on 25th January 1893.

This monument is erected by a large number of subscribers who revere the memory and value the works of this eminent servant of God!"

There are many more curious things to see and to absorb in both the Church and churchyard and it is all too easy to lose track of time when taking pleasure in this spiritual refuge.

The Cowper and Newton Museum is situated alongside the Market Place in Olney and is a truly interesting place to while away a few hours.

Step back in time with William Cowper, letter writer and poet, translator of Homer and explore his home, his life and find out what made this man so famous and loved by so many around the world.

Witness for yourself how and what life was really like in Olney over the years.

There are many things of interest on display: whatever your age and taste there is something for everyone.

Olney's Museum

Formation of the Museum
How it all began

On the **22nd July 1890**, the Buckinghamshire Archaeological Society sustained a temporary museum, mostly containing Cowper and Newton relics, at Etolia House, now Courtney House, Bridge Street, Olney.

Thomas Wright, a local schoolmaster, historian and author, saw an opportunity and attempted to set up a committee dedicated to finding a more suitable and permanent place to keep the Cowper and Newton artefacts, preferably the poet's former home, Orchard Side.

Sadly his idea was not well received, only a few showed some enthusiasm but generally there was a lack of local support. However, determined to keep the subject very much in the public's eye, Thomas gave lectures locally and wrote newspaper and magazine articles, which consumed much of his daily life.

In **1892**, his efforts were backed up by the publication of " The Life of William Cowper " and even more so when on the **24th January 1893**, the remains of John Newton and his wife, Mary, were brought from London to Olney.

Thomas was a well-educated man, strong in his faith and dedicated to his cause, although he must have had feelings of despair at this time, but he was not prepared to give up. With the centenary of Cowper's death fast approaching, he put the matter before a Parish Meeting but yet again he was met with a frustrating lack of enthusiasm – he could feel and see this important part of Olney's history slipping away right before his own eyes.

But then events took an unexpected turn for the best. On the **21st of September 1899**, Mr W H Collingbridge, the current owner of Orchard Side, bestowed an unexpected but very generous gift upon Thomas and the people of Olney. Mr Collingbridge had been closely following Thomas's cause over the last few years and had admired his focus and dedication and since Orchard Side was a second home for him, he came to a decision that it should belong to the people of Olney, and it's history and memory preserved, and so it came to pass. Orchard Side was bequeathed to the Town and Trustees were appointed to manage the new Museum and preparations were made for the centenary celebrations that lay ahead.

The big day arrived, **April 25th 1900** - Centenary Day of the poet's death and a day in which William Cowper was celebrated and remembered in Olney. The Town was gaily decorated, a triumphal arch was erected and banners displaying " God made the Country " and "He who lives to God alone" were hung from the arch.
Children from Weston Underwood and Olney, preceded by the Town Band, marched to the Market Place where Miss Evans delivered an address," Cowper and his love for animals" and the children ended the ceremony by singing, " God moves in a mysterious way ".
It was an impressive sight and, according to one local newspaper, people living as far away as 20 miles were reported to have travelled to Olney and assembled in the Market Place to witness the event and to participate in the celebrations.
Mr W W Carlisle MP officially opened the Museum and this was followed by a public meeting in the Congregational Church, in which Mr Collingbridge presented the Deeds of Orchard Side to the newly appointed Trustees. The celebrations were then drawn to a close with a service at the Parish Church.

History of the House

Orchard Side can be dated back to 1700 and is now better known as the Cowper and Newton Museum. Despite appearances, the Museum was originally two separate cottages joined by a central archway. When William Cowper lived at Orchard Side, his companion Mrs Unwin took the eastern side of the property, Gilpin House.

Behind the house are two beautiful gardens that have been host to numerous events held over the years and are well worthy of a visit. At the rear of the gardens is the quaint little 300-year-old Summerhouse where William Cowper wrote many of his verses, as well as many hymns with John Newton. Also in the garden is the Viper Barn and if you read further you will find out how that got its name.

Owners and Tenants

Orchard Side was owned by and rented to many different people over the years. But the most notable occupant was William Cowper, who rented the house in 1769; with his companion Mrs Unwin who resided in Gilpin House next door.

Owners

1700   Little is known, though the house has been dated to this period because of the inglenook fireplace in the kitchen.
1769   The Rev George Smith and his wife Mary own the house and it stays in the family until 1815.
1815   Mrs Smith sells the house at public auction to Robert Andrews.
1829   The Andrews children sell the house to clear their father's debts and James Hale Talbot becomes the new owner.
1854   The trustees of the late James Hale Talbot sell the House to Mr W H Collingbridge.
1900   Mr W H Collingbridge presents the house to the townsfolk of Olney and

Orchard Side becomes a Museum.

Tenants

1750   John Witney, John Marston and
John Palmer.
1769 – 1786   William Cowper and Mrs Unwin.
1786 – 1815   Daniel Raban and John Wykes.

Other Uses

In **1800**, local teacher, Thomas Haddon, was looking for a suitable site for his school and Orchard
Side was available to rent and turned out to be
perfect for his purpose. The school was partially
furnished from the sale of several of Cowper's
artefacts and was successful for many years.
However, due to a family tragedy in **1839**,
Thomas Haddon gave up the school and by the
time of his death in **1854** it had become the Dame
School.

A Guided Tour

It would not be fair to the Museum to share all of

Cowper's writing desk.

its secrets with you because, for one thing, they need visitors
and, for another, a personal visit is the only way of doing justice to this special historic monument. Nevertheless, the following is a short mouth-watering tour.

The Parlour

As you enter this room, you cannot help but feel that the occupants of the house are

still here as the room is decorated in colours that would
have been in the height of
fashion in the late **1700s**.
Pictures and personal effects
are still in the room and
carefully preserved for the
visiting public to see.

One particular personal item
of William Cowper's in the
room is his writing desk,
made for him by his cousin
Johnny Johnson. In his day
letter writing was almost the
only form of communication,
even locally, and being a man of letters, this piece of furniture played a vital part in

Cowper's life. The desk, more like a cabinet, contains pigeon holes disguised like book spines, for separating his correspondence. Some of the spines still have names printed on them, including, William Wilberforce, Lord Carrington, Lord Dartington and Lord Thurlow.

This is also the room in which Cowper wrote many of his works, two of the most familiar being, "God Moves in a Mysterious Way" and "The Task".

Standing in the room and sensing the atmosphere, it is easy to appreciate the source of this inspiration -

" Now stir the fire, and close the shutters fast,

Let fall the curtains, wheel the sofa round,

And, while the bubbling and loud hissing urn

Throws up a steamy column, and the cups,

That cheer but not inebriate, wait on each,

So let us welcome peaceful ev'ning in".

William Cowper

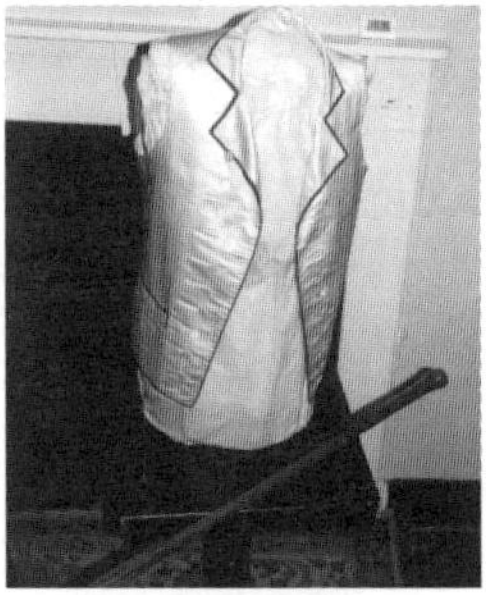

The prints over the fireplace are those actually chosen by the poet for this spot and it's remarkable to think that these prints have been here in exactly the same place for the last 300 years.

Cowper's sofa, or the Charles II day bed c1860, is also on display and became famous through a whim of Lady Austen. She wished that Cowper would extend his talents by writing in blank verse, all of which was very new to him. Initially reluctant, he eventually said that he would oblige but only on condition that Lady Austen would give him a subject. Her reply was,

"Oh, for you can never be in want of a subject, you can write upon any, - write upon this sofa!"

And so he began,

"I sing the sofa. I who lately sang Truth, Hope and Charity

Now see repose upon a humble theme".

The Costume Gallery

This was Mary Unwin's room when she lived in the house and the room now contains a number of period costumes. There is also a sofa in this room, which is draped with

William Cowper's bedspread this sofa was used on many occasions by the poet to read his works to Lady Throckmorton when she visited Olney.

Some of the other items on display...

The Rev. William Bull' s - Travelling Cloak.

Lady Austen's Presentation Dress

A now much faded dress that was originally a deep russet red and worn by Lady Austen when she was presented at court to King George III. It was later altered and reduced in size for a child of the local Grindon family.

Please note

Some of the items displayed throughout the museum are subject to change without notice. If the item you are looking for is not on display please contact a member of staff who will be very happy to assist you with your enquiry.

Ten other areas of interest to visit:

1. The Kitchen

A traditional kitchen with an inglenook fireplace c1700.

2. The Hall

A room whose front door was rarely opened and which housed many of Cowper's pets.

3. The John Newton Room

A room dedicated to the ex-slave trader and his life.

4. The Trade Room

Filled with local curios and tools of the trades from past businesses in and around Olney.

5. The Gordon Osborn Room

Visit the dinosaur and find out more about archaeology in the local area.

6. Lace Displays and History

Discover more about the lace trade in Olney and the impact it had on the Town. Numerous samples on display, even YAK lace.

7. The Gardens

Filled with plants, shrubs and vegetables, some of which can be dated as far back as **1800**.

8. The Summerhouse: in the garden

Visit Cowper's **300-year-old** garden house.

9. The Viper Barn: in the garden

And how it got its name.

10. The Shop

A perfect place to find mementos of your visit.

The Gardens

William Cowper was a keen gardener for many years and knew his plants well. He found the garden a constant source of solace and encouragement to him, especially during his many bouts of depression.

It was a restful and happy environment for him; for here he was free from the nearby screaming of children and the incessant barking of dogs. Many of his observations and references on nature were inspired from this natural habitat, and are reflected in his poetry and letters.

There are actually two beautiful gardens at Orchard Side, both of which are abundantly filled with interesting species. The Flower Garden, which is the closest garden to the house, has numerous plants, shrubs and flowers, some dating back to **1800**. Many of them are labelled and seeds, collected from the plants, are on sale in the shop.

The gardens are often used for hosting fund-raising

events. One of the most popular has been a Georgian Garden Party, held in the summer when hopefully the weather is favourable. With cream teas, poetry readings, some apposite music and a casual stroll through the gardens in full bloom and all their glory, visitors are contentedly transposed to centuries past.

In 1994, with a generous grant from the Carnegie United Kingdom Trust, a restoration programme was started. The aim was to recreate a garden entirely of plants that grew in Britain prior to the poet's death in 1800. The project is still on going and is being achieved with highly expert, though voluntary, workmanship. These dedicated volunteers, as well as providing gardens that are attractive to behold throughout the year, take cuttings, seedlings and seeds for re-planting and any excess goes into the shop for sale (and they do not last there for long!).

The paths were retained during the restoration, ensuring that the whole garden is accessible for wheelchair users. The plants are clearly labelled, large black print on yellow background, to assist the partially sighted and those who need that little extra bit of help when it comes to small print...

The Flower Garden is also home to the Parish Pump, which originally stood on the Market Place, and the stone ball from Sheil Hall is also on display.

The Viper Barn

The Viper Barn in the courtyard is within a few yards of the house and was aptly named after an incident with a Colubriad (Latin for snake). Cowper recorded the incident in a letter to William Unwin on Saturday **3rd August 1782.**

"Passing from the greenhouse to the barn, I saw three kittens with a fixt attention at something, which lay on the threshold of a door nailed up.
I took but little notice at first, but a loud hiss engaged me to attend more closely, when behold! A Viper, the largest I remember to have ever seen, rearing itself, darting its forked tongue, and ejaculating the aforementioned hiss at the nose of a kitten almost in contact with its lips".

The Summerhouse Garden

The furthest garden from the house, the Summerhouse Garden, is situated behind a stone wall and is approached through a separate gate. On entering through the gateway the first thing one sees is the stunningly beautiful 300-year-old summerhouse, hence the garden's name. This summerhouse measures 5'9" x 5'5" and was originally built around 1700 as a smoking room for Thomas Aspray, the local apothecary. There is a secret trap door in the floor, which hides an area once used for storing precious medicines and tobacco. The signatures and graffiti on the ceiling can be dated back to 1800, the time of William Cowper's death. Visitors viewed the summerhouse as a shrine to Cowper and many left their signatures as a sign of respect. However, today this practice is strictly forbidden!

In this garden, vegetables, soft fruits and even medicinal plants are grown and proceeds of any sales are ploughed back into the gardens. Beyond the southern boundary fence is Guinea Orchard and then there is the Old Vicarage, once the home of Olney's famous Curate, the Rev John Newton, the writer of Amazing Grace. Cowper and Newton were close friends and they spent a great deal of time in each other's company. Between them they paid the owner of the orchard, Mrs Aspray, a guinea a year (about £1.05) for the right to cross the garden. When Cowper left Orchard Side for Weston Underwood the gateway between the gardens was closed and this southern garden was let out to various tenants. It was not until 1919 that the Museum was able to buy the Summerhouse Garden from Gordon Osborn, a local Butcher, for £450.

William Cowper

In brief....

William Cowper lived at Orchard Side for 19 years with his deeply religious companion Mrs Mary Unwin. He was one of England's great letter writers and poets and during his lifetime he translated Homer and became world famous for his literary work.

Cowper suffered from anxiety and depression most of his life, which may have been caused by his mother dying when he was only 6 years old. This could be the reason too why he constantly sought female companionship; he became engaged several times but none of these courtships went further than that and he never married. Although he had no children, he looked upon and treated Mary Unwin's children as his own.

William was a keen gardener and had an expert knowledge of plants, much of which is reflected in the observations on nature in his works. He also loved animals and had many pets during his lifetime; but he was particularly fond of his hares, Tiney, Bess and Puss.

William Cowper died at the age of 69 and is buried in East Dereham churchyard in Norfolk but his fond memory is still alive and strong in Olney.

Some of the people in his life.

His mother: Ann Cowper

Ann, daughter of Roger of Donne of Ludham Hall, Norfolk, died giving birth to William's brother John when William was only six years old.

His father: The Rev John Cowper

Rector of Berkhamsted and Chaplin to King George II.

A companion: Mrs Mary Unwin

Mary Unwin was a deeply religious woman who was probably looked upon by William as either a surrogate mother or an older sister. William and Mary never married but spent 31 years in each other's company.

Close friends: The Rev John Newton

Ex-slaveship captain and Curate of Olney's Parish Church, John and his wife, another Mary, spent much time with William and Mary and the four were good friends. While John was in Olney, he and William wrote hymns, both separately and jointly, which became the **"Olney Hymns"**. Their friendship continued for many long years, even after both had left Olney.

An acquaintance: Lady Ann Austen

Sister- in-law to the Rev. Jones of Clifton Reynes. Lady Austen rented the first floor of the Vicarage in Olney so that she could spend more time in William's company. Lady Austen encouraged William to develop his skills and continue with his work. She was also credited with inspiring him to write John Gilpin and the Task. Lady Austen is

132

said to have been deeply in love with William but he never reciprocated so she left Olney in 1784 and went to live in Bath. There she married and eventually went to live in France, where she spent the rest of her days.

A cousin: Lady Harriet Hesketh

Formerly Harriet Cowper and at one time William's fiancée. She was well known for her visits and her ability to make William happy and giggle. She was also able to lift his spirits when he suffered from one of his many deep periods of depression. Harriet went on to marry Sir Thomas Hesketh but during her marriage she always maintained a close eye on William and was rumoured to have offered financial help and assistance to him on many occasions.

Cowper's Love for Animals

William Cowper loved animals and, as already mentioned, kept many pets during his time at Orchard Side. The following is taken from the "Treatment of Hares", which was inserted by William Cowper in a gentleman's magazine in **1881**. It makes for an interesting read, confirming his affection for the four-legged creatures.

"It was 1774 and being much indisposed both in mind and body, incapable of diverting myself either with company or books, and yet in a condition that made some sort of diversion necessary. Some children in nearby Silver End had acquired a small hare, which was approximately 3 months old. These children constantly teased the poor animal and the hare grew leaner each day. The father of the children had noticed this too and realising that this poor creature would not be able to withstand the taunts for too much longer, offered the creature to myself.

I willingly accepted my new prisoner, perceiving that in time and with the correct management this creature could be tamed. My neighbours knowing of my great pleasure for the creature offered me more; infact I had so many requests I could have stocked a paddock! I finally undertook the care of three and I named them, Tiney, Puss and Bess, and contrary to what you might think, they were all males.

On arrival of my new friends I immediately set about and built them their own houses and even installed a special feature that would catch their droppings, thus keeping them sweet and clean at all times. Their water bowls are also strategically placed so as not to overset them into their beds. I notice that all three are very protective of their surroundings, so much so that when a carpet burn on the fire rug had been repaired, all three scrutinised the repair on many occasions.

I give them full range of the hall so they can play their merry games and amuse me with their cheerful spirits. After supper they play in their parlour until such time that they are tired, it is at this point that they then retire to their beds. This rule has never lapsed on any occasion; they are very particular in their own ways.

I care very much for their diets and I feel I cater well for their needs. They are particularly fond of sow thistle, dandelion, lettuce and vegetables all of which I grow in the garden. They will eat fresh corn, but not the ear, which I find most peculiar consider-ing how greedily they eat their oats. They are also very fond of the Musk plant, which grows in abun-dance in the garden. I also give them fresh bread. Whilst on the subject of dietary requirements, I came across something that I hadn't experienced before. I was cleaning the fine silver sand from the birdcage one morning and replenishing with fresh, when I noticed that all three hares had started to help themselves at an alarming rate to the new sand".

On the hares themselves...

"Puss lived for 11 years and 11 months and would often leap into my lap for care and attention. He liked to be carried like a baby and would often fall asleep in my arms. He used to raise himself onto his back legs and nibble the hair on my temples; he did this on many occasions. I remember the time that he was sick, which lasted about three days. During this time I nursed him better and was gratefully thanked by the creature licking all of the fingers on my hand until he was fully satisfied. His favourite place was the cucumber vine in the garden, and after breakfast I would often carry him out and place him here, where he stayed for many hours chewing in a sheep like fashion. He often wanted me to join him in this restful spot and would indicate his intention by scuffing at my knee or biting the bottom of my coat and trying to drag me away. I have such fond memories of him and miss him very much.

Tiney lived for 9 years and was a very different character from Puss. He was very surly in his ways but he did have a mean sense of humour and was most of the time a very agreeable companion. However, I remember a time when he was sick like Puss. I nursed him back to good health but this time my efforts went unrewarded.

Bess, it is not known when Bess was born, he had much confidence and character and was easily tamed; he was also very strong and fearless, yet sadly died very young".

John Gilpin

John Gilpin was a comic poem written about a linen draper who, when setting off on his yearly holiday, was beset with problems from start to finish. Cowper first heard the tale of John Gilpin from Lady Austen, who recited a similar version to him during one of his many bouts of depression. It worked, and he immediately began working on it, albeit in a crude form whilst in bed. He later finished it off in his summerhouse, developing it not only as a poem but also into a standard ballad to be sung to the tune of Chevy Chaise.

On the **14th November 1782**, the Public Advertiser published the work as by an anonymous author. Public readings were carried out by a well-known actor of the time, John Henderson, and it was not long before the poem became famous and very popular. One London firm was reported to have sold 6,000 copies alone!

Many wondered who the real John Gilpin was. Was he based on someone locally? And did he really exist? There are two theories but no definite answers. One theory was that John Gilpin was a linen draper who lived in Cheapside, London and died on **11th May 1791**, aged 98 years. The other that he was a member of the Honourable Artillery Company of London; but he could have been both, of course. The ballad is allegedly based upon an event, which happened in the 1700s, but, even today, the identity of the real John Gilpin remains somewhat of a mystery.

Cowper himself did not rate John Gilpin very highly and considered it one of his more minor works; hence publishing it anonymously. Even after admitting to being the author he never liked the work and eventually refused even to have it read in his presence. But both adults and children have loved the story and it has been re-printed in more than 100 editions and translated into many languages. In **1931**, Olney carried out a re-enactment of the poem, which was recorded at the time by Pathe News. The Bull Hotel became

The 1931 re-enactment.

the Bell for the day and Harry Armstrong, the local lace dealer, was John Gilpin - and the horse really did gallop away!

An Amusing Tale: Cowper and the Hairdresser

Mr Wilson, a hairdresser, was in the habit of going to Cowper's house to shave the poet, who on these occasions was generally silent. It should also be noted that Mr Wilson was Cowper's wigmaker.

On one particular day the shaving routine was not conducted in such silence. Mr Wilson departed his house in a hurry to be punctual for his appointment, knowing that Cowper was due to dine with Lady Austen that day at Clifton Reynes. He had specially prepared Cowper's wig the night before but being in a hurry himself, he told his man to follow him with the wig. When the shaving had finished, Cowper suddenly exclaimed:

" Oh, Mr Wilson, my wig! "

To which, Wilson, who was not short of wit himself, quoted in reply from the ballad "John Gilpin",

" I came before your wig was done
But, if I well forebode,
It certainly will soon be here-
It is upon the road".

" Very well applied indeed, Mr Wilson", said the poet with a smile.

The Museum today

Old buildings whilst a valuable asset, can also be a liability in terms of operation and maintenance, and Orchard Side is no exception. The Trustees of the Museum have preserved the building diligently over the years, maintaining the building to a high standard. Today, however, maintenance is not enough. New and changing regulations require superior amenities for disabled visitors and educational facilities at a better level than demanded in the past. At the same time, conservation and heritage requirements are stricter, which often entails more expensive materials having to be used with enhancements and repairs. An application was submitted to the Heritage Lottery Fund in 2002, which would have provided sufficient funds for a complete restoration and development to modern standards. However, despite being very costly to the Museum in both time and money, the application was rejected. In consequence, the Trustees needed to revise plans and work towards the improved goals in stages over a longer period. Some grants have been obtained and some works have been carried out but more needs to be done.

The Olney Town Council, who are the owners of the Museum, have also contributed financially in the past few years and the Trustees have been successful with many fund-raising events. However, being able to meet the continuing demands of maintenance plus forthcoming regulatory requirements whilst, simultaneously, attempting to increase numbers of visitors and sustain running costs at existing levels, requires wholehearted dedication from all involved to keep the Museum alive. It would be a pity to lose this priceless Town asset after more than 100 years of success.

Aims and Needs Today

1. Meet the exacting Health and Safety standards.
2. Increase the visitor numbers and generate more revenue for repairs.
3. Further improve the facilities for the disabled.
4. Provide a facility for Educational Development.
5. Develop the museum as a heritage amenity for the town.

As already intimated, it is not easy to juggle all these balls in the air at the same time, especially when the Museum relies almost entirely on volunteers. There are only two paid, part-time staff, the remainder, (Trustees, Friends and a host of other supporters) give their time freely. And without being too irreverent, the majority of this remainder is the upper age bracket and there is the utmost difficulty in finding younger volunteers to give of their time.

What needs doing ....

1. Level land at the rear to make safer access for wheelchairs.
2. Provide an educational area, for visual aids etc.
3. Provide more office space for the custodian and assistant.
4. Provide an area for Trustees' and other meetings.
5. Provide space for archival material, (presently housed at Aylesbury).
6. Provide a covered area in the courtyard for functions and events.

The urgency and the costs!

The first two items are statutory requirements, which are long overdue. The first has been partly achieved near the house but more needs to be done when funds of, a few thousand pounds, are available.

Items 2 – 5 cannot be achieved within the existing space available in Orchard Side and Gilpin House. However, the Museum does own a cottage to the rear of Gilpin House, which could provide sufficient space for these items. But the cottage needs to be rented to cover running costs as it produces nearly 25% of recurrent income. Something like £6,000 a year would need to be found to release the cottage for these items, in addition to costs of conversion, which again is another, few thousand pounds. Item 6 would be a large project costing in excess of £100,000. However there would be the possibility of hiring out the area for sizeable meetings, functions or events. If the Lottery grant had been approved, all these items would have been covered and would now have been in place.

It's hard going and ongoing and it needs desperately some help!

Some really easy ways you can make a difference.

Pay them a visit

How many people in the Town can say that they have visited the Museum? If every family were to take their visitors into the Museum, say twice a year, the revenue on admissions from that alone would more than treble the current level. But it is not just the money; you would be showing off your gem of a Town and its rich history to enviable visitors in just an hour or two. The Town has much to be proud of, a great deal of which is contained in the Museum.

Support their events

Throughout the year the Museum hosts numerous fund-raising events. These include a Cowper and Newton Day, a Burns Supper, parties and dinners, raffles, quizzes and dances to name but a few. All these events are organised to raise funds for the purpose of keeping the Museum afloat but they also provide wonderful entertainment and enjoyment for the participants and there's always more room for support.

Make a donation

Donations to the Museum can be made by cheque in favour of the Cowper & Newton Museum. Further information can be found on their website www.cowperandnewton-museum.org

Do you have any spare time to help this very needy cause?

The Friends

Friends of the Cowper and Newton Museum are divided into two main categories. The first are those, from both near and far, who pay a modest annual subscription and in return obtain free entry into the Museum and receive the quarterly Bulletin free of charge. The second pay and receive the same but, in addition, give valuable practical help in the day-to-day running of the Museum. That includes serving in the shop, helping in the garden and with visiting groups, and assisting with the main fund-raising events. Not least, they run the catering side of events, providing thirst-quenching cups of tea, delicious cakes and other delicacies. Furthermore, the Friends organise their own coffee parties and other events to raise monies, which they accumulate for donating particular items of need, such as the cabinets for the new kitchen.

The group belongs to the British Association of Friends of Museums and to date there are about 90 Friends and this number is growing – but never fast enough! The representative Committee of the Friends holds regular meetings to keep abreast of happenings in the Museum and to plan and organise forthcoming events. They also publish the Cowper and Newton Bulletin, which is on sale in many places throughout the town. Anyone interested in making new friends, expanding the mind and devoting a small amount of time and attention to a very needy and worthy cause, would be warmly welcomed. A simple call to the museum is all that is needed.

The Cowper and Newton Society

The Cowper and Newton Society was formed in 1901 and, apart from a few dormant years, the Society has prospered and is in a healthy condition in Olney today. The main aim of the Society is to maintain public awareness in William Cowper and John Newton and to encourage the publication of unfinished manuscripts or scarce work relating to Cowper and his circle.

Subscription for membership in 1901 was just 7 shillings every two years and this entitled new members to free admittance to meetings plus a copy of the publication that was printed every two years. Over a century later the Society still meets on a regular basis and the aims and objectives remain the same. The Society hosts talks, dinners and events for all interested comers, whether members or not and any money raised is accumulated and eventually donated to the Museum for a particular need.

The Society is always on the look out for new members; they are a friendly well-mixed group of all ages, eager to give newcomers a warm welcome. The subscription today is a little higher than 7 shillings every two years – but not much more and it does entitle you to free admittance to the Museum.

Biographical Table: The Reverend John Newton 1725 - 1807

1725	July 24th	Born in London and baptised at Old Gravel Lane.
1732	July 11th	His mother dies.
1733		His father re-marries.
1735		He is sent to a private boarding school in Stratford, Essex.
1736	July 24th	Serving on board a ship that is under his father's command. 5 voyages are made to the Mediterranean.
1742	December 12th	First acquaintance with Mary Catlet, aged 14.
1744	February 24th	Impressed as ordinary seaman on H.M.S. Harwich.
		Moves from Royal Navy ships onto a merchant ship, The Pegasus, which is involved with the slave trade. Newton is working in West Africa (Guinea Coast) for a factory buying slaves. He falls out with his employer and becomes enslaved himself. He is rescued and returned to England via the Greyhound.
1748	March 10th	He encounters a violent storm at sea which led him to pray for the first time since his mother's death.
	March 21st	Newton's conversion followed from the aftermath of the storm.
1750	February 1st	He marries Mary Catlet at St Margaret's Church in Rochester.
	June 28th	His father dies whilst swimming in the Hudson Bay, Canada.
	August 11th	Undertakes his first command, the Duke of Argyle, a slave ship, which is taking, slaves from Sierra Leone to Antigua. He makes a second voyage as a slave ship captain on his ship the African.
1754	May	In St Kitts he is introduced to Captain Alexander Clunnie who introduces him to his faith.
	November	Newton suffers from some sort of fit and his sea career comes to an end.
1755	August 19th	He gives up the sea for the post of Surveyor of Tides in Liverpool.
	September 14th	Begins studying for the Church.
1758	December	The Bishop of Chester refused to ordain him.
		Newton takes leave of his position in Liverpool and accepted instead a temporary charge of an independent meeting house in Norwich. The Earl of Dartmouth becomes his patron.
	February 26th	Lord Dartmouth offers Newton the Curacy of Olney - he willingly accepts the position.
	April 29th	Newton is ordained into the Church of England by the Bishop of Lincoln.
	May 27th	He takes up position as Curate in Charge at Olney's Parish Church.
	August	An Authentic Narrative is written.

1767		Newton makes the acquaintance of William Cowper and Mrs Unwin and it is suggested that they all move to Olney.
	August 14th	William Cowper stays with the Newton family whilst Orchard Side is made ready for his arrival.
1769	Spring	Newton begins weekly prayer meetings in the Great House. He and Cowper write hymns for these meetings.
1773	August 12th	William Cowper has a breakdown and stays with the Newton family for 8 months. The Olney Hymns are published. 282 were written by Newton and 66 of them by Cowper.
1780	December 19th	Newton preaches his first sermon as Rector of St Mary's, Woolnoth, London.
	January	He preaches for the last time at Olney. He moves to London to become involved with the anti-slavery movement.
1785	December 7th	First counselled William Wilberforce, who wished to resign from the House of Commons - Newton dissuaded him, persuading him instead to fight for the abolition of slavery as an MP. He gives evidence from first hand experience to a committee of the Privacy Council investigating the slave trade.
1790	December 15th	His wife Mary dies from cancer at the age of 62. His niece and adopted daughter, Betsy, keeps house for him until 1801, until Betsy is admitted to hospital.
1800	May 2nd	Preaches at the funeral of his friend William Cowper, who is buried in the Parish Church of East Dereham. Betsy recovers from her time in hospital and later marries an optician, although she still kept house for her Uncle. Newton is almost deaf and blind but he stills continues to preach.
1806	March 5th	He makes his last entry in his journal.
	October	Preaches for the last time at a charity service to raise funds for the widows and wounded sailors on the anniversary of the battle of Trafalgar.
1807	March	British slave trade is abolished by an act of Parliament.
	December 21st	His health had deteriorated greatly and as he lay dying he jokes that he is " packed, sealed and ready for the post". According to William Jay, who was with him during his final hours, his last words spoken were; " My memory is nearly gone but I remember two things, That I am a great sinner and that Christ is a great saviour!"
	December 31st	Newton's funeral was attended by more than 30 ministers who have travelled from far and wide to pay their respects. His body was laid to rest in the crypt of St Mary's, Woolnoth, London.
1893	January 25th	Due to construction work on the London underground, Newton and his wife's remains are removed and re-interred at Olney on a cold and bitter morning.

Biographical Table: William Cowper 1731 - 1800

1731	November 15th	William is born at the Great Rectory, Berkhamsted, Herts.
1737	November 13th	His mother dies whilst giving birth to his brother, John. William was only 6 years old at the time.
1738 to 1740		Attends Dr. Pittam's boarding school in Markyate Street, Herts. Here he is severely bullied and tormented, his persecutor was later found and expelled.
1740		Took lodgings in London. Educated at Westminster School.
1742		Here he catches small-pox.
1748	April 29th	Admitted to the Middle Temple.
1749	May	Left Westminster School and spent 9 months in Berkhamsted.
1750 to 1753		Trained in London as a solicitor.
1753 to 1754		Engagement to Theodora Cowper abandoned. Moved to Middle Chambers where he had his first nervous breakdown, which lasted about a year.
1754	June	At the age of 23 he was called to the Bar.
1756	July 9th	His father, The Reverend John Cowper dies.
1757	April 15th	Admitted to the Inner Temple but has another breakdown. Returns to work at the House of Lords as a clerk to the private committees and finds his offices are being investigated for corruption. Depression sets in and two more attempts of suicide are made.
1763	December	Admitted to Dr. Cotton's, Collegium Insanorum Clinic, in St Albans.
1764	July	On the road to recovery, converts to Evangelicalism.
1765	June	Left St Albans and acquired lodgings in Huntingdon to be near his brother John.
	September	Whilst establishing himself in his new surroundings he visited a local church and formed a new friendship with the Reverend Morley Unwin and family.
	November	William moves in with the Unwin family.
1767	July	A terrible accident happens. Reverend Unwin was thrown from his horse and died.
	October	William and Mrs Unwin decide to leave Huntingdon and look for alternative lodgings in either

Olney or Emberton.

Year	Date	Event
1768	February 15th	Orchard Side in Olney was deemed a suitable option. The house had recently been refurbished to a very high standard and was also very close to St Peter and St Paul's Church. In addition to the location, the house was also blessed with a very large garden, which delighted William, as he was a very keen gardener.
1770	March 20th	William's brother John dies. William was left a small legacy but the loss of his brother proves too painful to bear and depression sets back in. He was nursed back to health by Mrs Unwin, who encouraged him to keep his mind occupied. Took heed of this advice and in collaboration with the Reverend John Newton he began Olney Hymns. William Cowper and Mrs Unwin became engaged. William is again suffering from depression and the engagement is called off.
	August	William attempts suicide again and moves to the Vicarage to be cared for by the Reverend Newton- he stays for 8 months.
1774	May 23rd	William moves back to Orchard Side.
1779	February	Olney Hymns is published - 66 of them he wrote himself.
1780	December	The Progress of Error and Truth was started.
1781	Jan- Mar	Table Talk and Expostulation written.
	Spring	Charity written.
	July	First acquaintance with Lady Hesketh.
	August	Retirement started.
1782	March 1st	Poems by William Cowper of the Inner Temple Esq. was published.
	October	John Gilpin was written.
1783	October	The Task was started.
1784	May	First acquaintance with the Throckmortons.
	October	The Task was completed.
	November	Tirocinium completed and the translation of Homer commences.
1785	July - Oct	The Task is published.
	October	William begins corresponding with his cousin Lady Harriet Hesketh.
1786	November	An invitation from the Throckmorton family provided William and Mrs Unwin with a tenancy for the Lodge at Weston Underwood.
	November 29th	News was sent of the death of Mary Unwin's son, William Morley.

1787	Jan-June	William is greatly affected by the loss of May's son and attempts suicide again, but was foiled by Mrs Unwin who found him and cut the rope from around his neck.
1780	September	He started the translation of the Odyssey, which helped keep his mind occupied.
1790	January	Cowper meets his cousin, John Johnson.
	September 8th	The translation of the Odyssey was sent to the press.
1791	July 1st	The Translation of Homer was published. He receives £1000 for it but remained dissatisfied with the results and ended up spending the best part of his life correcting it.
	September	Translation of Milton's Latin and Italian poems had begun - later completed in March 1792.
	December	Mrs Unwin suffers her first stroke.
1792	May	Mrs Unwin suffers a second stroke. William is now beside himself with worry and anxiety for his companion.
	Autumn	Renewed depression sets in.
	November	Lady Hesketh arrives and takes charge of the household.
1794	January	William is suffering again and has another breakdown.
	April	William is granted a pension by the King of £300.
	May 17th	Mrs Unwin has a third stroke.
1795	July 28th	William and Mrs Unwin take comfort and rest with John Johnson.
	August	William and Mrs Unwin set off for Mundesley by Sea to gain refreshment and improve their health and minds.
	October	They are now staying with friends at Dereham Lodge.
1796	December 17th	Mrs Unwin dies at Dereham Lodge. She was buried in Dereham Churchyard on 23rd December
1797	November	After nearly a year of mourning he starts his revision of the Translation of Homer.
1799	March 8th	Homer now completed.
	March 19th	The Castaway is started.
1800	January 31st	Cowper is treated for a dropsical order that came on very fast. His friend, Sir John Throckmorton encouraged him to carry out some exercise but William was too frail and weak and couldn't manage it.
	February 22nd	William is confined to his room - he is now too ill to move.
	April 25th	William's dies aged 69.
	May 2nd	He is buried in the parish of East Dereham.

Clifton House, High street Olney c. 1920.

Historical Houses

Historical Houses

Olney is without a doubt home to many fine houses, many of which you will see predominantly down the High Street, but also throughout different places in the town. They are all beautiful in their own way, each having its own unique character, but many of them are valuable reminders and templates of building methods used a long time ago, and rarely seen and no longer used today.

As with any property in Olney today the houses on sale fetch very good prices, it's a good place to live but there are some properties that are more valuable than others both in monetary terms and historical content.

In the late **1950s** Sir Nikolaus Pevsner, Art and Architectural historian made a unique contribution to the execution of English Architecture in England by assessing the country's buildings county by county. He recognised the importance of compiling a historical record of the buildings in each town that he visited, describing their style and noting any unusual features. In **1960** his book entitled, The Buildings of England: Buckinghamshire". It is said even today that if your house has a favourable mention by Sir Nikolaus, a 10 % increase is automatically added to its current sale value, which is always a nice thing to know.

So, is your home one of them?

His walk started at the southern end of the town and some of the buildings mentioned no longer exist today but I have decided to leave them in and record them as they were mentioned- you never know....

"To the north of the Bridge and on the western side are the first of many stately late Georgian houses of the town. Built of stone

as most of them are, **Bridge House** *has five bays, three storeys, a round-headed doorway and a broken pediment (also recurrent motif).*

The Mill is of four storeys, partly stone and partly brick, and includes the **Millers House**, stone, of five bays and three storeys, with the same type of doorway inside, according to O. Ratcliff and H. Brown. The house is home to some very fine fireplaces that came from the Great House that once stood nearby.

The street bends round the churchyard and to the north of this stands the **Vicarage**, built in **1767**, long and two-storied, with irregular fenestration. Then on the other side is **Courtney House**, early c19th century with broad tripartite windows, after that the street joins up with that from the Bridge.

At the front of the former **School of 1847**, are two big shaped gables with a big window under each of them. Opposite this is a graceful **c18th century shop front (Wine Bar)** and to the right of this is a **house of 1717** with odd lunettes above the upper windows. After this Weston Road joins from the West.

The Vicarage.

School of 1847.

Courtney House.

House of 1717.

The Wine Bar.

The Almshouses of 1819 are two-storied, of chequered brick with a central pediment; twelve tenements in all. The Market Place opens on the east and overlooking it from the west is the **Bull Hotel** with an early Victorian or slightly earlier front with a white and black deep-columned porch.

In the Market Place is the most important which stands on the South Side; Cowper's House now the **Cowper and Newton Museum**. This is probably mid-Georgian, red brick not stone, vertical bands and angle rustication in vitreous bricks. Six bays, three storeys with raised oblong panels below the windows. Two doorways with pulvinated friezes and pediments. Behind the house in Cowper's garden is his tiny unassuming **Summer House**; direct connection existed in the past from here across the one field to the Vicarage garden.

Side streets interrupt the High Street, which gives it the most gratifying continuity, of which the following houses deserve notice.

No. 6 High Street (Francis Jackson Estates) is of three wide bays, three storied, with the centre oddly emphasized by three tiers of pilasters. The doorway with slim gothic triple shafts, the windows were no doubt tripartite.

No.14 High Street (original house no longer here, replaced by Wine Rack) is of the early **c18th**, of three bays and two storeys, with quoins and with tripartite windows to the left and to the right of the pediment doorway. Above the doorway is a window with side volutes.

Opposite is **Olney House**, a fine mid-Georgian house of three bays and two storeys. The whole of the ground floor is rusticated; the doorways of the type already met and to the left and to the right are Venetian windows, also a

Venetian window in the left hand annexe (Now Evelynn House, No.15 High Street). After that are several more nice door cases.

On the other side of the street and a bit further up is **Clifton House** (no longer standing), with five bays, three storeys and with a door case as seen before.

Finally, and on the west side is **Orchard House**, c18th century like its neighbour to the right which has a pretty door case with some gothic detail. A. E. Anderson of Northampton designed the front of Orchard House in **1904**".

I didn't know that....

Olney House

When the above house became two properties in the earlier part of the **19th Century**, the annexe to this house became known as No.15 High Street, which is now known as Evelynn House. This left the bigger portion of the house as No.15a High Street. The Allen family who owned the house at the time decided that Olney House would be a far more suitable name and so it was changed an given a far more suitable name: Olney House.

Clifton House

Some parts of the house did survive and are still about in the local area. The door case and the actual door are still about today and are wonderful reminders of a beautiful house that once blessed Olney's High Street.

The Bull Hotel

In 1883 the Bull Hotel it was used by the Inland Revenue. William Cowper used the Bull as a safe house when his staff became ill with smallpox.

Orchard House

Sir Nikolaus Pevsner was so impressed with the house when he visited Olney he asked the current owners Bob and Dorothy Soul if he could study the original plans of the house with the intention of passing the knowledge he gained onto his students. The letter that follows is the reply that he sent back to the owners when he returned the plans to them.

A copy of the letter recieved from Sir Nikolaus Pevsner

BIRKBECK COLLEGE
(UNIVERSITY OF LONDON)
MALET STREET
W.C.1
LANGHAM 7941

DEPARTMENT OF THE HISTORY OF ART
HEAD OF THE DEPARTMENT
N. B. L. PEVSNER, C.B.E., Ph.D.

From:-
18 Gower Street,
London W.C.1.

28th October 1958

Dear Mr Soul,

Thank you very much for your letter of 20th September enclosing the original plan of the alterations to Orchard House. This has been most interesting

Yours sincerely,

N. Pevsner

R.F. Soul Esq.,
Orchard House,
Olney,
Bucks.

The Great House 1642 – 1833

Situated right by the river, on the southeastern side of St Peter and St Paul's Church, once stood a magnificent property known locally as the Great House. Rumoured to have been built on the site of the Old Parsonage c1503 it was also mentioned in a Charter in the reign of King Henry 7th. King Edward 4th was also reputedly taken prisoner here.

The house was a substantial e-shaped building with three storeys and many gabled ends; and would have certainly provided a grand panoramic view of the countryside from any of its many mullioned windows. The house was built by William Johnson Esq. who settled in Olney around **1642** and was used as the family home for many years.

Other local records show that William Johnson also owned and occupied the Vicarage, which is very close by, and whilst living there he also undertook extensive building work to the property making the house into the size it is today.

The Great House had many uses and with the church so close to the house it was ideally suited for the overflow congregation that attended whilst John Newton held his services. Other accounts show that it was also used as a school on Thursday afternoons, with John Newton acting as the teacher.

The last known occupier of the house was the Rev. H. Gauntlet, Vicar of Olney **1815-1833**. After his death the house fell into disrepair and after standing for 161 years it was ultimately demolished. However not all was lost. Some parts of the house were saved and are scattered around the town; some of which can still be seen today. These wonderful items are the only evidence and reminders left of the house's existence.

The next time you pass the entrance to St Peter and St Paul's church take a closer look at the two stone columns and the gate that's there. These were rescued from the house and put where they stand today by local workers at the time of the house's demolition. The fireplaces from the house's main hall as mentioned by Sir Nikolaus Pevsner earlier were also saved and a new home was found close by.

There is no trace of the house today, nothing can be seen, and the land it once stood on is now privately owned. However, past droughts have been kind enough to reveal where it once may have stood which was very, very close to the river's edge and by now any evidence of its existence would have been well and truly washed away by the river a long time ago.

79 High Street: The Old Cinema

Situated 60 yards from the pavement and at the northerly end of the High Street is old cinema. Built by local grocer Lewis Thompson the cinema started off life as the New Hall Picture House, which hosted many concerts, meetings, dances and election meetings. By 1919 it was converted into a silent cinema and was renamed the Electric.

As you would have entered through the front doors of the cinema, the pay desk (which was a vestibule and table) stood on the right hand side of the room and the projection room was over the front porch.

All of the seats had their own prices depending on what you wanted and of course what the pocket could afford.

Later, and with new owners Mr & Mrs Clifford, the cinema continued to host many enjoyable evenings with Madam Clifford (a most regal lady by all accounts) often playing on the piano whilst the film was showing.

Mr Chapman was employed as the projectionist who was well known to the paying audience for his methodical routine of putting the last film away and in its box before getting a new one out. This would always take him a few minutes to do, so watching a film was never as fast flowing as it could have been. Ironically though, this poor mans carefulness didn't help much when it came to showing "The Eternal Flame" in which he some how managed to badly burn his fingers...

Ownership of the cinema then passed over to J. B. Poyntz who conducted his affairs in a very strict and orderly way. He didn't like people eating whilst watching the film as he felt it spoilt other people's peace and quiet. Here, here! I agree!

In 1927 a building application was submitted to the council to increase the current seating capacity of the cinema to 286. The General Purpose Committee at the time refused the application on the grounds that the escape passages at the cinema were not substantial enough to cope in an emergency and as a result the application didn't go through. Despite the set back improvements were made to the cinema. A new floor was installed as well as a purpose built operating room which was installed over the main entrance.

The cinema then passed into the hands of Mr Webster a film distributor who, amongst other things, arranged for twice-weekly coaches to the cinema from Newport Pagnell to Olney.

On the **28th June 1952** the last film " Three Little Words" with Fred Astaire was shown and its days of being a cinema finally came to an end. As well as being a cinema, No.79 High Street has also had an involvement with the Boot & Shoe Trade, the Lampshade Factory and until more recently offices and now a beauty salon.

Thatched Houses

Have you any idea how many thatched houses are left in Olney today? I know of 5 and wondered if you know of any more.

Their Location

1. The Sun – Weston Road
2. Maltings -Corner of East Street
3. East Street
4. The Allotments
5. Orchard House Garden

1

2

3

4

5

Olney's Workhouse

No longer standing today but situated at the southerly-end of the town, just opposite the Church Hall, once stood Olney's Workhouse and Tan Yard.

The earliest known reference to the Workhouse in Olney can be dated back to a survey of Workhouses undertaken nationally in **1724**. This survey listed the Workhouse in Olney as being under the occasional superintendence of Mr Mathew Marriott. Although the daily running of the Workhouse was given to a Master who, in Olney's case was paid £16 a year for keeping he Workhouse in tip-top working condition.

Olney's Workhouse had 30 residents, many of them old and incapable of financially of supporting themselves, so for them; the Workhouse was their only option.
For those that did reside here, the Workhouse provided food and clothing and a place to sleep. A hot meal was served twice a week and two small bushels of beer were also allowed. The bread supplied came from John Soul's Bakery and they were also allowed cheese.

But life wasn't easy and you don't get something for nothing and for those that lived at the Workhouse, they were expected to earn their keep by working and undertaking the orders as set down by the Master.

It was a bleak and miserable existence in the Workhouse and for those that died whilst under the Workhouse charge, the bodies were given a simple ceremony by the Church and placed in unmarked graves in the Churchyard.

A sample of some of the rules and regulations set down in the Workhouse.

1. If you refused to work the hours set down by the Master you would have been sent to a House of Correction.

2. Anyone pretending to be sick would have the contents of their stomachs and other related samples thoroughly investigated and checked. If anyone was found to be lying, severe in-house punishment was administered.

3. Anyone found begging or charring would be sent to Bridewell.

4. In summertime you woke at 5.00am and went to bed by 9.00pm.

5. If caught you were caught stealing another person's property, you were severely reprimanded.

Orchard House, High Street Olney.

Satisfy your curiosity and see for yourself what lies behind this grand facade, and imagine what life would have been like for the well to do nearly 100 years ago.

The present owners Mr Bob and Mrs Dorothy Soul have very kindly given permission for the publication of never before seen pictures of their private family home.

Orchard
House

History and Ownership

Situated in Olney's wide and attractive High Street is a fine Edwardian House with 17 front windows, 15 fireplaces and an acre of private and exquisite gardens, which

stretch as far back as West Street. The house has had an interesting and well-documented life and were formerly two houses dating back to **c1780**. But today, Nos 67 and 69 High Street are now better known as Orchard House.

This pretty, little low-thatched house, with it's fine off centre archway **c1690**, is still standing today in the back garden of Orchard House and was listed in local records as No 67 High Street and was used as a school by Walter Pennington-Storer, **c1850**. Walter only lived a few doors away, No 75 High Street, but after two years of living there, he ended up marrying the girl next door, Jane Hull and a short time later the gardens were combined.

The 1859 House.

Going back a few years earlier to **1854**, the Great Fire of Olney had destroyed many houses and upset many people's lives and Jane's father, William, was one of these. The fire had damaged his house, No 73 High Street, and he was forced to move out whilst it was re-built- and so he moved into No 67.It was also around this time that William also acquired No 69 High Street.

When William died his widow, Elizabeth continued to live at No 67 but sub-let No 69 out to various tenants. Elizabeth died in **1863** and her son-in-law, Horace Hummel, inherited her estate. By **1886** Horace's son, another Horace, decided to cultivate the large garden that the house is blessed with today. Some years later Horace senior sold both of the properties to Mr J. W Mann, a shoe manufacturer from Wellingborough Road.

Beautiful carvings.

By **1904** J. W Mann was undertaking many major alterations and extensions to both the front and rear of the property as well as making many fine alterations inside. It was at this time that the two properties were joined and converted into one large family home. No expense was spared on the conversion and many of the internal features incorporated at the time are still in pristine condition today.
J. W Mann died in **1951** after 46 years of residency and the house was sold to Mr Bob Soul on his 40th birthday, and is still the current owner today.

So in the 100 years since the conversion of this property from two houses in to one there have been only two families living there. And after getting to know the house, it's not difficult to understand or see why Bob and Dorothy have never, ever, had the urge to move.

Orchard House in the 21st century

Today's Owners

Today's owners are Mr Bob and Mrs Dorothy Soul whose family connection with Olney can be traced as far back as **1669**. The family were continuously in business and living in the Town, mainly trading as bakers and lace dealers and many of the descendants were called John.

Local records show that a "John Soul" supplied bread to the local workhouse (see the previous chapter) but he died on the **4th January 1853**, which strange to tell was the same day as the local Stanza / Fire Ballad was written about the recent fire in the Town by Thomas Aspray (reproduced at the end of the chapter). The oldest surviving picture of a close relative is of Cornelius Soul, who died in **1732**, aged 67, whilst climbing Mount Everest and this treasured memento proudly hangs on the wall in the main hall of Orchard House.

In **1912** the last of the " John Souls " died leaving no heir to inherit the family concern so the baking business was closed down. Meanwhile, John's younger brother Fred (founder of today's business) had set himself up at the present site, in High Street South as Souls Garage.

Going back a few years earlier, to **1909**, Fred had started a business, and was advertising as a Motorcycle Agent and Repair shop, which later went on to sell prams. The business soon developed and before long it had incorporated cars even buses, the latter of which undertook schoolwork and private hire. Fred died in **1934** aged 53 leaving two sons, Bob and William, and one daughter, Irene. Bob and William were both young men when they took over running the family business but with plenty of hard work, strong values and commitment to customer service they expanded not only the garage but also the coaching business into what they are today.

As already mentioned, on Bob's 40th birthday he purchases Orchard House. This proved to be a wise move as he and Dorothy went on to have a large family, 6 children of their own and, at the last count 17 grandchildren and 6 great-grandchildren! Not only has the house been a wonderful family home to Mr and Mrs Soul they have been active members of the community. They have opened the up the gardens of Orchard House to the public on numerous occasions, as well as playing host to many fund raising events held there.

Bob has spent 25 years as President of the Olney Cricket Club as well as being

President of The Olney Tennis Club, Olney Badminton Club, and Olney Town Football Club. He and Dorothy have also sponsored and supported many other projects, charities and associations within the town over the years and the activity doesn't stop there - there has also been some serious car-collecting going on in the interim period.

Over the years Bob has managed to acquire a fine collection of rare vintage cars, many of which have taken part in public ceremonies and have been hired out for local weddings etc. The **1912** two seater Vinot et Deguingand was regularly featured in the television series of "Upstairs, Downstairs". The **1908** Vinot et Deguingand has also had many parts on television in various programmes and both cars could often be seen on a sunny day parked outside the front of the house for all to enjoy and admire.

The house has been lovingly cared for under this owner's care - nothing has been tampered with or altered since the conversion in **1904**. It is such a beautiful house, which has aged very gracefully, which if anything, has further enhanced its character and charm. Only essential light and general maintenance work - which all homes need from time to time has been its only need.

With the family business continuing to grow and, in keeping with the family traditions, Bob's two sons, David and Andrew, now run the businesses, allowing Bob and Dorothy to enjoy their long-awaited and well-earned retirement!

Welcome to Orchard House

When Orchard House was converted in 1904 into the fine Edwardian house that we see today, the architect for the conversion, Mr A. E. Anderson, incorporated wherever possible a garden element into his design and build.

Orchard House Plans.

Bob is in the fortunate position of possessing of the original architect's drawings, which in them selves are a precious works of art. The plans show in great detail the architect's wish to reflect aspects of the garden, and specific detail in particular rooms have been painted green to reflect this.

At about the same time as the work was being carried out on Orchard House, Anderson was co-designing and working with Charles Rennie Macintosh on a house in Derngate, Northampton, which is another historically important building of interest. Charles Rennie Macintosh was a renowned designer of windows and the ornately designed glass in Orchard

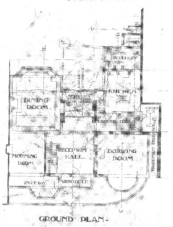

GROUND PLAN.

House would seem to indicate that he might have had some involvement or influence in this project too, the dates match up and we know that he was in the area at the time. The Charles Rennie Macintosh Society in Glasgow does not list Orchard House among his work but it would seem worthwhile for them to investigate its inclusion.

As with a number of the houses along the High Street, this one is also blessed with wells, two of them in fact. One is soft water for bathing and the other, hard water, is for drinking. Orchard House was also the first house in the town to have electricity, by means of a petrol - driven generator installed by the previous owner. The heating for the house was – and still is - provided by 15 strategically placed coal fires and in bygone days, during the winter, the Bell Boy did little else but kept these fires going. The temptation to install central heating has never been an option as it could harm the wooden panelling installed throughout the house. The structure of the house means that the house is cool in summer and warm in winter and all that is necessary these days for supplementary heating is the odd electric heater here and there.

As regards the ornamental frontage of the building, the name Orchard House is carved in to the stone portal above the door and the fruit and flower motifs appear in several places.

The tree-shaped cast iron railings surrounding the house had a lucky escape during World War 2. Other houses in the Town had to relinquish theirs so they could be melted down for the war effort – as happened all over the country. But the precious railings at Orchard House were listed and therefore thankfully exempt from this necessary but unfortunate regulation.

The Vestibule

Once inside the house you are immediately aware that there is no traffic noise – it's all so quiet. The house is warm and welcoming, the latter aided by a voluptuous angel blowing his horn to greet you. It's as if he's announcing your arrival into this great house, and it's a lovely gesture. He is in fact an ornately designed light fitting which is ideally suited to this area of the house.

Then, as you pass through another door, you step into the main hall. This hall can sometimes be glimpsed from the pavement when the two entrance doors are open and it whets the appetite of those who would love to sneak inside for a closer look. Once inside though, at first glance it is an awe-inspiring sight, there is just so much to take in, it's very difficult to know where to start, one can only gaze and attempt to try and absorb the true splendour of it all.

I feel as if I have stepped back 100 years in time, and the Olney that I have just come from, simply doesn't exist yet.

The Main Hall

The feature fireplace is as the architect, Anderson, designed it in 1904, as are the fender and the fire irons. The copper hood is also original and is ornately designed to reflect the garden.

The canti-levered, galleried staircase is a magnificent and exquisite piece of architecture that couldn't have been easy to install. The spindles that surround the staircase from top to bottom are in the design of William Morris and the stair-rods, which one does not often see these days, show little sign of wear, and despite being 100 years old, they are all still in perfect working order.

The previous owner, Mr J W Mann, had the impressive chandelier with its plethora of glass orbs, fitted during his occupancy and it's interesting to note that even though the lighting throughout the house is still 50 volts, the house is now powered from the mains via a transformer; which reduces the power back down to the house's original voltage.

Here we have another feature, the rocking horse, which is kept in one corner and looks perfectly at home in this hall. He's in very good condition considering his great age but surprisingly, even after years of being ridden and having its tail pulled by the children, grandchildren and great grandchildren, it doesn't have a name.

The parquet floor is the original floor and is host to a Herringbone design, which was very fashionable at the time of the alterations- but this one has an additional and unusual feature included in it. Around the edges of the floor, which are covered by deep-piled rugs are tramlines, which, I have been reliably informed, served two purposes. Firstly, they were to keep the rugs in perfect place and secondly, they were a path for the servants. The servants were only allowed to walk on these outer areas and not on the rugs. Oh no, one simply couldn't allow the domestics' mucky boots to walk all over the master's very expensive rugs - that just simply wouldn't do! How times have changed; attitudes today need to be more liberal towards those domestics that one is lucky enough to find nowadays!!

Hiding in one corner is a mysterious oak panelled and glass door, which could easily be missed but it's just too tempting not to open. However, open it as I did and there I discover a well-kept, un-altered, Edwardian gentleman's cloakroom with an original suite in the style of Thomas Crapper- a really wonderful sight and not what I'd expected at all!

There are numerous things to see in the hall, all of which carry much interest. It's a truly lovely start to my tour but which door should I go through next? I'm beginning to have an affinity with Alice in Wonderland...

The Drawing Room

This comfortable and inviting room is known affectionately as the drawing room. One appreciates how spacious the room is when you eventually notice the baby-grand piano nestling in one corner, ready and waiting for its keys to be tinkled.

The bay fronted glass window is ornately designed in the Art Nouveau style and seems to stretch on forever and is a brilliant source of light. The coloured glass, which is typical of the style that runs throughout the house, really enhances this room. The colours filter through the sun even on the dullest days, and the room begins to fill up with magical hazy clouds of pinks, blues and greens. The best time to be in the room to witness this is first thing in the morning when the sun is up, it's then that the whole room lights up with a dancing, cascading display of colours and shapes. It's a truly wonderful sight to see and my first experience in this magical room was on such a morning.

There is also a delicate pink theme running throughout the room. There are pink flowers woven into the original Donegal carpet and pink marble surrounds the fireplace surround, and the ceiling mouldings have also been painted pink. The colours may have faded slightly but that's only to be expected in such a permanently bright room and all of the fixtures and fittings in here are the original ones as fitted in **1904**.

The architect also designed the mantelpiece in the room, which is decorated with acorns and leaves that appear so real; its very tempting to try and pluck one out. The pink marble surround complements the brass hood, which again has an engraving on it in a classic

design incorporating the garden.
The ceiling in this room has an interesting
story attached to it. In **1904** J W Mann
commissioned an unknown French crafts-
man to undertake the redecoration and
design of the ceiling. The artist set a condition that none of the family, not even the
servants, were allowed in the room until
his work was finished and he was totally
satisfied with the end result. This condition
was very reluctantly agreed to and the

Frenchman made sure that the door always remained locked; and as promised family
and servants nervously stayed clear. Many anxious days passed and eventually the
family were invited in for a viewing - fortunately for him and everybody concerned,
they all liked it!

The Morning Room

Although somewhat smaller than the drawing room, the
morning room is nevertheless spacious and contains some
interesting features. Its bay window, like that of the drawing room, faces on to the High Street and the window seat
below, which is ornately designed with its original uphol-
stery, is a very comfortable place to perch and watch the
world go by.

The room has been recently redecorated with William
Morris wallpaper, the pattern of which draws influence
and design from the galleried staircase outside in the hall.
The maid's bell is still fixed to the wall and is in good
working order but sadly the maids no longer come running
nowadays!

The Dining Room

This wondrous room overlooks the garden and
takes your breath away on entering. As you draw
back the tall heavy velvet curtains the garden
immediately beams back a breathtakingly beautiful chocolate box view and, regardless of the
weather, it's simply stunning and you immediately recognise why the house was given its name.

In the room itself, the prominent eye-catching feature is the ceiling with its mouldings,
which are up to six inches deep in places, depicting motifs and elaborate scenes of fruit

and flowers. The wallpaper is the original, hung in **1904**, and is still in excellent condition, especially when you consider its great age. To preserve this and other treasures in this naturally bright room, the curtains remain drawn when the room is not in use.

A saltbox that hangs on the wall was a gift from the Allen family (Garard & Allen Solicitors). The tea urn (also in its retirement) is from the Cowper Tea Rooms, now better known as the Olney Wine Bar. And one cannot help but wonder when looking at it, how many cups of tea it has poured in its lifetime and for whom; no doubt it would have a great many stories to tell.

In one corner a very large picture hangs of Olney Church **c1900**, painted by William Wright, father of Thomas Wright who founded the Cowper and Newton Museum. The dining room furniture was custom made, also about **1904**, and is familiarly decorated with carvings of fruit and flowers.

The oak panelled doors and architraves are all elaborately moulded and the brass door furniture is designed, like so many other things, in the art nouveau, fruit and flower style.

It's easy to understand why this is one of the current owner's favourite rooms. Its grandeur is breathtaking and its beauty captivating and once visited, this room will stay with you forever.

The Party Room

The Party Room is situated on the first floor and was originally known as the Billiard Room. It is without doubt the biggest room in the house and can well accommodate a large party, as its name suggests.

The ceiling does not bear the ornate garden scenes typically depicted in other ceilings throughout the house. Instead it contains representations, history tells us, of an unidentified local Masonic lodge that Mr Mann may have been connected with when he lived here- perhaps lodge meetings were held in this room?

The fireplace in this room is very, very large and unfortunately the picture does not do it full justice. This was one of the features mentioned by Sir Nikolaus Pevsner when he visited Orchard House and he regarded it as being historically important and an extremely fine accompaniment to the room.

On one side of the room is a large slumbering oak chest, which was possibly used at one time to store games and equipment. It was made by the previous owner's son and left as a gift for Mr and Mrs Soul and it serves as a nice reminder of the Mann family and their conception of this fabulous property.

The Garden

This extensive garden, of nearly an acre, stretches through to West Street and is bursting with a multitude of plants, trees and flowers of all varieties. It's immaculately kept and has gardens within gardens as well as some un-expected hidden features. The dedicated gardener, yes there's only one, seems to work miracles in maintaining this enchanting piece of paradise right here in the heart of Olney, it's a sizeable area to manage and yet this wonderful effect seems easily and effortlessly achieved.

The Greenhouse

Local building company, W. T Revitt, erected this large and sturdy edifice around **1904**. The company is no longer trading today but descendants of the family still live in the Town baking bread and delicacies instead of building grand and beautiful greenhouses.

The greenhouse was built in traditional style of its time and over the years it's developed it's own character and charm, even today, 100 years on, its still has it's original glass. The windows still open and the original winding mechanisms are also in good working order.

The greenhouse is situated very close to the kitchen, which makes it very handy to nip out for some hothouse niceties, and it's still well stocked today with many herbs, plants and soft fruits.

The greenhouse is a splendid haven to retreat to. It's warm, it's relaxing, and you can feel its bygone atmosphere embrace you as you enter which makes it a truly delightful spot to browse about in, and an ideal place to spend some good quality, quiet time in – a perfect bolthole.

Mr. W. T. Revitt, Building Contractor, Newton Street, Olney

The following was an extract taken from Oliver Ratcliff's " My Look Around Olney", 1907

"Mr. W. T. Revitt commenced business in May 1903 as a horticultural builder in a small workshop in the High Street. In 1904 owing to an increase in business he found it necessary to build the present commodious premises.

Mr. Revitt is holder of certificates under the City and Guilds of London Institute and has practical experience in most branches.

The constructional parts of buildings, drainage, sanitary work and decorating were added to the business at the request of several friends, and having a thoroughly efficient staff at his command, he is prepared to execute any of the above works in the most satisfactory and up-to-date manner. He will be pleased to furnish estimates and give advice for anything in the way of modern dwellings, public works, and all contracts appertaining to the advertisement.

High-class joinery, conservatories and greenhouses still constitute his specialities, while your repairs will not be despised.

Specimens of his workmanship may be seen in the decorations and alterations carried out in the following places in the town".

Cowper and Newton Museum, Olney: Museum front façade decorated and renovated.

Cowper Memorial Church: Front façade renovated and redecorated.

Messrs. Eastman's Ltd: New shop front and fixtures.

Mr W. E. Moss: New shop front and fixtures.

Mr T. H. Murton: Shop front window fittings.

Mr F. W. Morgan, decorator: Alterations and new shop front.

New Chapel: Ravenstone.

And many other works, all of which show the high quality of the work executed by him.

Olney's Community Workers Past and Present

This final chapter of the book is dedicated to the Community Workers Past and Present and it is a somewhat different – yet relevant - local **WHO'S WHO** of Olney.

The aim is to create a small record of a selfless group of people who, by dint of dedication, hard work and sacrifice, have given and still give their time so freely for the benefit of the many well-established clubs, groups and organisations that exist in our community today.

It is all too easy to take such people for granted and, with time passing as quickly as it does, it is also too easy to forget. But it is safe to say that, without them and their efforts, Olney and the surrounding villages would not be such fascinating, and favourable places to live.

I fully appreciate that this is not a comprehensive list of those who have given their valuable time and service to the community over the many years and I apologise to anyone who may feel offended at being excluded.
I would be very happy to receive accounts of others' contributions, which would be included in any reprints; or, perhaps there is a case for publishing a separate WHO'S WHO for Olney?

Mr Peter Bebbington

Peter has lived and worked in Olney all of his life and has worked at Soul Garages for over 40 years. Still living in Olney with his wife Rosemary in the same house they had when they married. Here they brought up their two daughters, Martine and Lucy of whom they are extremely proud.

In his youth Pete was involved in various sporting clubs: football, cricket and hockey. He was on the committee of Olney Football Club and the Social Club and was involved with the fundraising to build a new club house in 1970.

In 1974 he became involved with Olney First and Middle schools both as governor and fund raiser . At one time the school board was a joint committee and eventually separated into two governing bodies. Pete gave 22 years as School Governor, 15 of these as Chairman of the Board, mainly at Olney First School.

The other great interest of his life has been the 27 years spent as a member of the Olney Fire Service. This has been a great part of his family's life. Over the years they have all helped raise money for the National Benevolent Fund. During his last 7 years of time with the Fire Brigade he was Officer-in-Charge of the Olney Station. These days life has taken a different route; now a proud grandfather time is often spent with the family as well as enjoying holidays to the more unusual destinations.

Mr Bill Bethune

Designer of the Olney entrance signs, flower beds, street improvements and instigator of the Market Place improvements. Private architectural designs include:
Rose Court Brasserie
Dagnall House extension
1 Market Place, Olney : redevelopment
Tennis Pavilion and many other building improvements in the town.
Committee Member of the Olney Chamber of Trade and the Christmas Lights sub-committee (as is Deirdre). Minutes Secretary for the Olney Branch Labour Party and Chairman of the Olney Festival of Arts.

Mrs Deirdre Bethune

I have been a Town Councillor since 1978. I wanted to be on the council so that I could make either a difference or at least be heard if I didn't agree with the direction things were going.

(I used to read of the council's actions in the paper after they had taken place and so too late for public input). During this time I have followed in the footsteps of others to be honoured as Mayor of Olney for four years.

I was a School Governor for the First and Middle school when it was a joint governing body and stayed on as governor for the Middle School when they got their own bodies and was chair of governors for many years.

Currently, I am Membership Secretary of the Olney Chamber of Trade, Trustee of the Cowper & Newton Museum and the longest serving Councillor on the Town Council. Bill and I were also involved with the Arts Festival with many other people who gave freely their time to the town. I am also Treasurer for the Olney Branch Labour Party.

Mrs Coral Bex

Having been in St. John Ambulance from the age of 18 it was only natural that when I moved to Olney in 1975 I made contact with the local division; it was a wonderful way of getting to know the town and its people. I took over the running of the cadets from Jean Minard until the 1980s and continued to build up and extend the Division's participation in training, duties and Competition work.

During this time I also joined the Olney Lace Circle and was for a time their secretary and, according to one of my bobbins, treasurer for a year. I contributed toward two of the lace pictures which are now displayed in the Cowper and Newton Museum, Olney.

I handed over the Cadet Division to Elizabeth Knight when I was promoted to Area and then County Staff but was still a frequent visitor to their meetings for teaching, examining and inspection.

I also taught many a First Aid course to willing townspeople and immensely enjoyed this part of my service. When I became County Badger Leader I ran the Brock Badger Set here in Olney, for six to ten year olds, helping them, according to their song, with " Absolutely everything a badger needs to know". We even entered a float in the Floral Fiesta with a wonderful backdrop which was painted by Leslie Hancon, who helped me run our set. We also served breakfast for the senior citizens in the Olney Working Men's

Club and went to the Great Party in Hyde Park, which the Queen attended.
As Personal Training Adviser Co-ordinator my duties included not only being an adviser but also arranging training for other Adult Personal Advisers. After 32 years with the Brigade I am no longer a member but am still a Serving Sister in the order of St. John as well as secretary of the Olney and Newport Pagnell Fellowship. The Fellowship was set up for retired members and anyone else who has ever been involved with St. John Ambulance.

I am now a trustee of the Cowper and Newton Museum here in Olney and spend time helping out in their shop, giving guided tours for groups and assisting with the Thursday coffee mornings which are held in the museum shop. I am also a member of the choir at the Parish Church and took part in the joint productions of the Roger Jones musicals " Saints Alive" and "From Pharaoh to Freedom" which were performed at the Sutcliff Chapel.

I am now entering into another phase and hope to play a useful part in the community but I feel that I have done no more than most, probably a lot less than some. My school motto was " Trust, Hope Serve" maybe this has coloured my attitude to life.

Mr Steve Clark

My involvement in the local community has been quite diverse, starting with a spell as a part-time worker at the Olney Youth Centre from October 1975 until March 1979. A move to the volunteer-run weekly Youth Club at Sherington followed.

My interest in conservation issues led to a period of involvement with Milton Keynes Friends of the Earth , including duties as Press Officer. Our greatest claim to fame was organising a " Day of Action " to protest about global warming on a day when the centre of Milton Keynes was impassable due to heavy snow!

In May 1992 I became a member of Olney Town Council, and was re-elected in 1996 and 2000. In my first year as Town Councillor, I became the Council's representative on the Management Committee of Olney Youth Centre, serving several years as Chairman and currently as Vice Chairman.

I was elected as one of the two ward members for Olney on Milton Keynes Council in 1996, and was re-elected in 1998 and 2002. I was nominated as an LEA representative governor at Olney First School, and have served on that body since. I also managed to complete a 3-year stint as a member of the Local Radio Advisory Council at BBC Three Counties Radio.

Other than trying to find enough time to do my " Day Job " my main interest outside Olney lies with Equine Welfare and in 1994 I was invited to join the Board of Trustees at Redwings Horse Sanctuary, Norfolk. In 1995 I was elected as Chairman, a post that I have been immensely proud to hold to this day.

Mrs June Davies

I first became connected with Willen Hospice as a volunteer working in their Day Centre. I spent one day per week there working mainly with cancer patients who came in on a daily basis. I started the day by collecting several of them from their homes in my car, and taking them to the hospice. Whilst there, I sat with them and chatted with them, helped feed them and also helped with Occupational Therapy for those that wanted it. I did this for about 16 years before retiring myself due to ill-health.

However, I still work for the Hospice in a fund raising capacity. The Hospice started a weekly lottery with prizes ranging from £1,000 to £10 and we collected a £1 per week from the contributors.

I have a round of about 70 participants, and I still collect their dues on a fortnightly basis. From time to time, some participants drop out, but I have been able to keep my numbers steady by recruiting newcomers to the scheme. I also run bric-a-brac stalls in aid of the Hospice on Pancake Days, Floral Fiesta Days, Dickens of a Christmas Market Day, when I also sell my home-made jams and marmalades.

Other Voluntary Positions:

I was Honorary Secretary of the Olney Archaeological Society for 12 years, and after a 2 year break as Vice Chairman I am now back as their Honorary Secretary. I am also a friend of the Cowper and Newton Museum and I serve in the shop on a regular basis. I do many other voluntary jobs, too many to mention.

The Late Mr Les Fairey M.B.E and Mrs Fairey

I came to Olney in 1947 and resided in Spring Lane, when Leslie was in employment with Mr. C. M. Allen, where on leaving school he became Mr. Allen's apprentice.
My husband, a native of Olney soon became involved in local affairs and was co-opted onto the Town Council, he later became Chairman, a post which he held for over 20 years. He also served on the Newport RDC and the Milton Keynes Borough Council and was the first Hon. Alderman of Milton Keynes and probably the first in the country.

Leslie was also instrumental in getting Olney Rugby Football Club going after the War and served 20 years as their President. Governor of Local Schools and concerned with Rennie Lodge Hospital, his proudest moment was when he went to Buckingham Palace to receive his MBE from his Royal Highness the Prince of Wales, for services to the community.

I joined the Women's Institute and acted as Secretary and President. Olney Wives' and Mothers' Club was also another one of my interests and I was their President for a number of years. I also assisted in the business of Allens of Olney and still continue to do so today.

Mr Edwin Horlock

My wife Joan and I moved to Olney in February 1984, just before Pancake Day. I was approaching retirement from full time employment and we had chosen to live in Olney for our retirement years. Having newly arrived we were keen to find out as much as we could of our new environment, the local activities and the Pancake Race Party in the Church Hall which was one of the first public events we attended. Little did I know then how involved Joan and I would both become in the Pancake Race in later years.

One of the reasons we chose Olney was the opportunity it gave us to participate in the worship at the Parish Church. I soon joined the Parochial Church Council and thus got more involved in many of the Church's activities.

In 1987/88 discussions were held about installing a sound reinforcement system and, because of my background I was asked to prepare an outline specification and make enquiries of a number of likely providers and installers of the equipment. The PCC chose to give this work to a company called Christian Communication Support Service. In discussion with Ron Hall, Director of CCSS, it transpired that the PCC could save much of the cost of the system if the actual work was carried out locally. I undertook to do this voluntarily and the system was installed in August/ September 1988; and has been looked after and added to by myself since this time.

One early addition provided the facility to record the services and concerts that took place in the Church. Often these audio tapes were duplicated and sold in aid of particular functions, especially the Shriving Service which is held every Pancake Day. A few years later Ron Hall came to Aspley Guise to install a sound system at St. Botolph's Parish Church. I went to help him and whilst there and in conversation, I mentioned that I had given some thought to a new amplifier design that could be controlled from anywhere in the church using a small remote handset. Rom immediately saw another important feature, the amplifier could then be placed anywhere in the church, in a locked and secured cupboard, away from meddlers and vandals.

In conjunction with another friend, who owned his own small electronics production company, the system was developed and emerged under the trade name EDVICRON (Edwin, Vic and Ron) and a lasting friendship ensued. Since then over 200 of these systems have been installed in churches mainly in the south-east of England, as the design is still unique today.

I was asked by the Elders at the Olney United Reform Church about installing a sound system. They eventually agreed to choose the EDVICRON equipment and I installed the system in November 1993, saving them the labour cost for installation.

A short time afterwards the Olney Town Council, who after seeing a demonstration of the URC system, decided to have a similar system installed at the Olney Centre. I happily agreed and this was carried out in March 1994, again I undertook the installation at no extra cost. Both of these systems were designed to meet some novel switching flexibility, enabling the system to be used in either of the two rooms or both rooms together using the remote control system, play and record facilities.

In March 1995 I constructed a special portable sound system for the Clifton Court common room, a room which is used for meetings. A nominal charge was made for some of the equipment used and I was only too pleased to donate my services to them. A similar arrangement was made with the Rugby Club in August 1996 when they decided that they needed to update their current system. In all of these cases I continue to give my services for any subsequent maintenance and repairs.

I started this piece by saying that Joan and I wished to participate in worship at St Peter and St Paul's Church, all of which I have managed to achieve as well as being the Church Warden in 1987 - 1992. The other significant contribution related to the church was serving on the Pancake Committee from 1985-1996. Firstly I helped John Hanson with much of the secretarial work but when he suffered a stroke in 1989, I took over the job of co-ordinating the events activities. At that time committee meetings were held at our house, it was at this time that Joan started to take more of an active part and helped me with the organisation. I continued with this role until Daphne Tate died, I then took over the role of Chairman and Co-ordinator.

During my time with the committee a number of new activities were introduced to enhance the presence of Pancake Day; for example prior to the main race, races for the children from both of the schools in Olney were set up; entertainment was laid on and market stalls were allowed to trade. We also aimed for a wider and greater media coverage and more ecumenical participation in the Shriving Service in the churches. These activities are now firmly established as being part of Pancake Day in Olney.

All of them have been added to encourage more Olney participation on the day and coincidently to raise contributions from the public (without making the event too commercial), thereby making a noticeable difference to the church funds.

Another important aspect of Pancake Day is the connection that it has established with folk in Liberal, a town in the south west corner of Kansas, U.S.A. That connection in 1949 is well documented elsewhere, suffice to say that it is still very strong some 55 years later. That link was initiated by Mr. R. J. Leete in Liberal and Canon Collins, local Vicar, Olney. On behalf of the committee I designed a plaque which R.J. Leete unveiled in Room 4 at the Olney Centre during a visit with his wife, Virginia.

Over the years many visits have been exchanged between the two towns and Joan and I were privileged to make the journey to Liberal in 1997 to represent Olney. We spent a few days there meeting their townsfolk and were also present at their pancake race, unfortunately Olney didn't win that year.

In January 2004 I arranged for a replica of the plaque in the Olney Centre to be presented to the newly opened " Pancake Hall of Fame " museum in Liberal. This plaque was also unveiled by RJ and Virginia Leete on Pancake Day 2004 and is now on display as another tangible link between Olney and Liberal. Olney didn't win this year either!

Though the Parish Church is the primary benefactor from the Pancake Day other organisations also benefit through sponsoring nominated runners and holding charity stalls on the Market Place. Many of the commercial organisations in Olney benefit indirectly from media coverage, publicity and people visiting the town generated by the event.

Mrs Joan Horlock

I moved to Olney with my husband in February 1984 having just retired as a Domiciliary Teaching Midwife in Huntingdon. I soon became interested in helping at the baby clinics held in Olney and continued to assist with these for about 10 years. Later I got involved with Meals on Wheels service delivering meals to the elderly in Olney and the local villages, again I did this for about 10 years.

Soon after we moved here, my husband Edwin became involved with the Pancake Committee and I helped him by canvassing prizes from the local shops and commercial premises, selling Prize Draw Tickets, helping to prepare the Pancake Day Prize Giving Party and the actual prize giving to the runners and Draw.
On behalf of the Pancake Race Committee, Edwin and I arranged to have some souvenirs of Olney produced, tea towels, mugs, plates etc. These were all sold in aid of the Committee's funds. I actually took the photos of the church, museum etc. which were then incorporated into the tea towel designs.

I have also accompanied Edwin as an Olney Representative to Liberal, USA on Pancake Day 1997.

Voluntary Work for St. Peter and St. Paul's, Olney Parish Church
When we came to Olney I became involved with Church activities, initially in helping with the collating and distribution of the Parish Magazine. At the behest of the vicar, I initiated several projects in the church which are still on-going although today they are now being done by other volunteers. These include:

1. The Bible Reading Fellowship using Daylight booklets, " Guidelines".
This first group met monthly at our house, now it meets monthly at Clifton Court.

2. Creating an awareness in and supporting the Children's Society in Olney. Acting as local secretary, distributing collecting boxes and arranging for the proceeds to be handed to the society. In conjunction with the society and the vicar I initiated the annual Christingle Service at the Church.

3. Encouraging couples' interest in Baptism of their children and following up that interest with the family in the early years of their children's lives. In association with this I arranged an Annual Party for the families with their newly baptised children.

4. Inaugurated the Church Kneeler Project and acting as liaison between the manufacturers and the church congregation, ordering kneelers as requested helping to design and making kneelers myself. There are now some 215 kneelers plus two lectern banners in situ at 1st January 2004.

Recognition for their response and effort should be given to the many people who have made the kneelers and also those who have donated money and their time to provide this magnificent display in the Church.

Mr John Joseph Kent

I was born in Olney on 29th November 1921 at No 10 Weston Road. I was educated at the Convent School, West Street, Olney from 1927 and then attended the Grammar School at Wolverton from September 1933 until July 1938. I sat for the Clerical Officer's Examination of the Home Civil Service in 1938 and was successful in being offered a permanent position as I had come within the first hundred out of 2/3000 taking the examination. I joined the District Audit Service late in 1938 and served in this service then appointed under the provision of the Local Government Act, 1933, until I retired aged 60 in 1981.

I enlisted in the Royal Air Force in July 1941 and trained as a wireless mechanic at Manchester University and R.A.F. Malvern and passed out in March 1942. Upon completion of training I was posted to Operational Fighter Command 13 Group Headquarters and served until 1944 in Great Britain, North Africa and Scilly on detachment. As an N.C. O. I was responsible for the service and maintenance of airborne V.H.F. radio equipment fitted to operational spitfires. Beaufighter (Night-Fighters) Mustangs and on one occasion Catalina flying boats on patrol from Sullom Voe base in the Shetland Isles (a base which is now used for North Sea oil landings). The airborne radio link enabled the operations room to communicate and control aircraft in action or patrol over the Atlantic Ocean for German U-Boats. In 1944 I was posted to Madras, India South East Asia Air forces seconded to Government of India and was R.A.F, N.C.O Representative at an Indian factory rebuilding and repairing, if possible by cannibalisation (i.e. making as many serviceable units possible from unserviceable parts), a classic example, being able to make a starter motor for a Liberator aircraft from three returned.

This factory was an off-shoot of a British firm in Chelmsford, Crompton Parkinson, wireless power units, starter motors, generators, magnets and aircraft equipment.

When I returned from R.A.F. Service back with District Audit I passed the Civil Service Executive Examination and then studied for three years to become a District Auditor. I was successful and became qualified in 1953 and was appointed as a District Auditor on 20th February 1956 and I served over a wide area of England and London carrying out audits of local Government authorities.

Olney at this time was a much smaller community than it is today and everybody seemed to know what was going on in everybody's lives and it wasn't long before the large brown envelopes which had H.M. Treasury, OHMS, stamped on them, became the topic of conversation. Many thought I was a spy because I worked for the Government, and that the brown envelopes contained information on future missions. Alas, this was not the case; the envelopes only contained course papers, marked papers and relevant writings!

I became a Trustee of the Anne Hopkins - Smith Almshouses, Weston Road, Olney in 1961 and I am still a Trustee today. Before the Almshouses were restored the buildings were in a very bad state of repair; 10 homes remained empty and No.43 had a Sycamore tree growing out of its roof. I handled all the paperwork and construction works for the refurbishment project which was completed in 1983 at a cost of £200,000 and financed almost entirely by Housing Corporation Grants. The Almshouses were built in 1819 as homes provided by Miss Anne Hopkins-Smith, a Quaker resident of Olney, her remains are interred at the rear of the Old Quaker Meeting House, which stood at the end of East Street in a small garden, the rest of which has since been re-developed.

I have also served for the following:

Formation Committee, Olney Floral Fiesta 1966
Olney Town Councillor 1964-1967 and 1984-1991
Co-opted committee member of the Milton Keynes Association of local councils and still am to date.
Internal Auditor of Weston Underwood Parish Council
Internal Auditor of Emberton Parish Council
Former Trustee and Treasurer of the Cowper and Newton Museum, Olney 1981-1991
Clerk of the Olney Feoffee Charity, still current
Committee member of the Olney Branch of the Royal British Legion 1998-
Poppy organiser 2000-2002
Branch Chairman 29th November 2002 - to date

The Late Mr Stanley Kitchener

Mr Stanley Kitchener although born in Lavendon has lived most of his life in Olney and now aged 92 must register as one of Olney's longest living residents.

Having two daughters, one being my mother, three grandchildren and five great grandchildren, all local, he must often ponder on how things have changed in the town.

Whilst too young to have served in the 1914-1918 war, during the 1939-45 war was in a reserved occupation and contributed to the town by Home Guard duties in the protection and care of all at home. He contributed to the country by working in the local brickworks maintaining production of necessary building materials to combat wartime destruction.

Travelling to work during this time had to be undertaken under your own steam, no public transport ran to the brickworks, but as a motor cyclist owner - seen here on his 1903s Aerial this was not a problem unless it broke down, then it was the pedal power of the pushbike to cover the 15 miles each way, despite the weather conditions and the blackout.

A very principled man, these were inherited from his father who had strong religious anti-war convictions, he has always been a keen gardener, a typical Kitchener trait and up until recently grew many of his own vegetables, with his grandson Nicholas now taking an active part in the tradition.

He has always enjoyed an interest in sporting matters, this being reflected in family involvement in Olney Rugby Club at the beginning with his father, Sam Kitchener's involvement here and in Bedford, to his grandson's involvement with the club in the 1980/90s.

Despite some of the grim times he has lived through he has always found the time to help others. Employed later in life by the Electricity Board he also worked for them in a welfare capacity supporting ex-employees, continuing this after retirement and, up until recently he still had some involvement.

Very much a family man he is always on hand if needed but has also found the time to be a good neighbour by taking friends less able than himself for hospital outpatient or other such appointments. Other than my obvious bias to his worthiness, so many who know him comment to me that he is a very nice gentleman and I do hope that he can achieve, or better the longevity of his uncle, Bluech Kitchener, whose name was given to the ever so popular Kitchener Centre here in Olney, and who by possession of an Olney birth certificate qualified as an authentic Olney Centenarian.

Mr Charles and Mrs Elizabeth Knight M.B.E.

Elizabeth joined Olney St. John Ambulance Division as a young mother wanting to know how to cope if her children had any accidents. Her husband, Charles undertook a first aid course soon afterwards, thus carrying on the Knight family involvement with the St. John Ambulance.

Charles became an officer with the Olney Cadets, then transferred to County Staff in a variety of posts over the years, including County Staff Officer for Cadets and C.S.O for Milton Keynes, and is currently in a personnel role for the Northern Area of Buckinghamshire. He also regularly acts as a casualty for the statutory First Aid at Work courses.

During the Queen's Golden Jubilee Year, Charles was invited to have tea with the Bishop of Oxford in recognition of his 50 years service with the Parish Church, much of which involved teaching young people bell ringing.

Elizabeth was content to remain at local level with St. John Ambulance, training cadets and eventually becoming Superintendent of Olney Division. Having trained a good team of young adults to take over the running of St. John, she decided to retire in April 2002, coincidently the same year as the Division celebrated its official centenary.

Elizabeth was awarded the M.B.E. for services to the community of Olney in the New Year's Honours List 2002, which acknowledged 30 years involvement as a Trustee at the Cowper and Newton Museum, including a 4 year period as custodian: and recognised the long association with the Parish Church of St. Peter and St. Paul's, during which time she has undertaken various different roles within the church.

Elizabeth is also a founder member of the Olney Lace Circle, which is coming up for its Silver Anniversary and being keen to see the equipment for this traditional craft still being available in the town, she took over an existing lace supplies business ten years ago.

Other interests include maintaining the Museum gardens, local and family history and lace making. Elizabeth is also an author, W. I. Speaker and leader of the guided walks around Olney. When asked how she manages to do all that she does, she is not ashamed to say that she does not do much housework as, " There are many more interesting things to do in life other than dusting! "

See Bibliography for Elizabeth's Knight's Publications.

"The Knitwits": Betty Pratt and Judy Underwood

Since Willen Hospice opened in the early 1980s my friend, Mrs Judy Underwood and I have been keen supporters. In the early days we held coffee mornings and cake stalls to raise money for the Hospice. In 1990 we decided to use what skills we had for knitting children's jumpers etc, to be sold at craft fairs, table top sales and anywhere else we could find. The Olney Pancake Race was one of our favourite venues.

We recruited a small band of helpers, whilst Judy and I concentrated on the character jumpers; Thomas the Tank Engine, Fireman Sam and numerous other types, our loyal knitters also provided us with baby clothes and all sorts of other goodies that could be sold to the public.

We decided quite early on to call ourselves the Knitwits, it raised a laugh and it did help people remember us. We carried on for 10 years and during that time we attended many toddler groups, play groups and nurseries as well as every fete in the immediate area. Whenever there was a chance to make some money for the Hospice, we were there.

We are very proud of the fact that some of our jumpers even went abroad; some as far away as Australia, America, Canada, even Ireland and France. Unfortunately, by 1999 the demand for hand knitted goods disappeared and we were forced very reluctantly to give it all up. However, we took comfort in the thought that over the years we have helped to raise almost £14,000 for the Hospice.

We have also helped with the collections in the village for Willen Hospice, The R.N.L.I. and the Royal British Legion. Today, we are still fundraising for the Hospice and we now run dances at the local Pavilion.

Jean Minard

In keeping with a family tradition I have managed to achieve roughly 40 years of Service to the St. John Ambulance here in Olney. Since my retirement in 1986 I have had an active involvement with the W.R.V.S, Meals on Wheels and serving teas and coffee at Woodhill Prison, Milton Keynes.

I also help those who are house-bound by returning their books to the local library as well as catering for their literary needs. As I have my own car I also drive those that are unable to do so to nearby hospitals for either out-patients appointments or relative visits.

I am also an active member of the Sutcliff Baptist Church here in Olney and my involvement with the Church has led me on to assist with the much needed voluntary work that is always needed as well as teaching at the Sunday school, all of which I enjoy enormously.

Mr Alec Morgan 1924-1996

Alec Morgan was born in Olney and lived there all of his life except for the five years he served in Europe and the Far East during World War II; for which he was awarded the " Certificate for Good Service."

Alec was a true Olneyite which is why he dedicated much of his life to serving the people and the town that he loved. He was an Honorary Secretary for 25 years for the Royal British Legion and during this time he helped increase the membership numbers from 70 to almost 200. Every year he organised the Remembrance Day Services and personally made sure that all Remembrance Day crosses were placed on the graves of the ex-servicemen and women, and on the War Memorial which is on the Market Place. He also compiled a register and photographic records of the backgrounds of those men from the town who gave their lives during World War II.

Alec was also a co-trustee on the officer list for the Odd Fellows Society and a Trustee of the Ann Hopkins Trust when the Almshouses were renovated.

He also served on the Parochial Church Council for many years and was Chairman of the Stewardship Committee and a Church Warden.

Also a Trustee of the Olney Feoffee Charity and eventually over a period of time ended up as their clerk. He was also a member of the then Parish Council during which time he served as School Governor.

He was an avid supporter of the town's sports clubs and was Vice President of the Olney Rugby Cub and the Olney Cricket Club. He also tirelessly supported his wife Mona with her fund raising for Willen Hospice.

Mrs Mona Morgan

Mona Morgan was born in Petsoe End, Emberton and has lived in Olney for more than 50 years. She is a State Registered Nurse and much of her community work stems from her love and interest in nursing.

She was a member of the St. John Ambulance for many years and was responsible for restarting the Nursing Cadets Division. For many years she has been very involved in fund raising for Willen Hospice and served on the committee set up in Olney for the purpose of fundraising for the Hospice through the League of Friends.

She had a small stall under her car port where she sold donated items; jams and marmalade all of which she made herself. She also organised coffee mornings in her garden with all the funds going to the Hospice, and for many years she organised the Willen Hospice house-to-house collections in Olney and was a volunteer in the shophere in Olney. As a trained nurse she has been called upon on numerous occasions to nurse terminally ill people in their own homes. She has also worked tirelessly for the Church over the years as a Sunday School Teacher and was also a member of the Parochial Church Council, Church Warden, Treasurer, Stewardship Committee member and bell ringer.

Mona has now taken over from Alec the task of putting crosses on the graves of the ex-servicemen and women at the time of Remembrance.

The Reverend Nigel Pond

Was the Rector of St Peter and St Paul's Parish Church, Olney from May 1993 to November 2003.Sadly, Nigel is no longer with us as he's enjoying a well-earned retirement in Suffolk with his wife Jose. However, during his time here he managed to achieve rather a lot for the church and it is for that reason why Nigel's contribution to the town has been noted and recorded in Heart and Soul.

Prior to his arrival the interior of the church was in a desperate need of updating. The church was cold and the lighting was inadequate. There was no kitchen, no toilet and building surveys had revealed that the main structure and fabric of the church also needed hefty care and attention. With no funding available for the work it was a matter of raising the necessary money themselves. Then, the late Mr Phil Cowley left a most generous legacy to the church and this was the start of the on-going and future improvements.

After numerous years of hard fund-raising and with the help of public donations the church now looks a very different place. A new central heating system has been installed which now makes the church feel much, much warmer as you enter. New lights have been fitted which look truly beautiful on or off and there is also a public gallery, a kitchen, even a toilet and all of this has been achieved during Nigel's time here.

Ask anyone who knows Nigel and many will say what a nice man he was and how good we was at doing his job. Nigel was also a guiding force to those that helped with the numerous projects in the church. He was an excellent communicator and a tower of strength when it came to supporting, guiding and encouraging others to continue with a project guiding and encouraging others to continue with a project when the end result seemed so far away.
Nigel's contribution to Olney and the church have been outstanding and his contribution over the years has far exceed those expected. His hard work and achievements over the years will be enjoyed and savoured by the residents of Olney for many long

and happy years to come and for that we would like to say a very big Thank you!

May the next part of Nigel's pilgrimage be that of a more relaxed pace but one that provides him and his wife Jose with as many great things as he has given to Olney.

Miss Ruth Plackett

I was born and bred in Olney. It's home even though I have spent many years overseas. Work entails being a full-time midwife over the border in North Bedfordshire.

Locally, I have been a member of St John Ambulance. My role as Divisional Nursing Officer since 1986 includes teaching care courses here and elsewhere in Bucks. Public duties in the Town include attendance at the Floral Fiesta and Shrove Tuesday's Pancake Day events.As a Christian I thoroughly enjoy worship and sing in the Parish Church Choir.

Much of me and what I have achieved through life has come from my parents to whom I owe an enormous debt of gratitude.

Mrs Margaret Plackett (nee Keen) 1905-1988

My mother came to Olney as the District Nurse / Midwife. She and my father, Cecil, loved sport and met at the tennis club. Dad was in the cricket team 1922, played for Olney Rugby Club 1923-1928, and was also in the bowls team for many years, where he was a good groundsman until 1941. Mum though preferred hockey and even played in the Olney Ladies' Hockey Team.

During the war years our home was registered as a Maternity Home. Women with no nearby family support came to have their babies without the need to go to hospital. The local midwife came to conduct the delivery and mum gave all the homely care needed and this service continued spasmodically until 1963!

Living in the vicinity of the Primary School, which is now the Olney centre, Mum's nursing abilities were used when any of the children needed immediate attention. Known by the Olneyites as Nurse Keen or Nurse Plackett, she was an active member of the St John Amubulance Division, being the Divisonial Nursing Officer who was awarded Serving Sister of the Order in 1973.

She has also helped with the Old People's Club, worked in Westlands and also support-ed Olive Rogers in her Maternity Home at West Farm, Emberton.

A stalwart member of the Women's Institute and at one time a committee member under the leadership of the austere Mrs Grindon, wife of the local doctor, she was also a keen member of the local drama group.

As a regular church-goer and at one time chorister she later became part of the team that polished and kept the church brasses in shining condition. Mum was always supportive, gave sound, sensible advice and had very high standards with no half measurers!

The Late Mr Alf Page

My late husband has always been eager to help out wherever or whoever he could in Olney. He loved having fun and spent much of his free time at the local drama group which was set up by him and a few others to have a bit of fun. Soon, the word had got round and more and more people began joining.

There was always a show put on for the Fiesta week which is held in the town, as well as numerous dances to assist with; he even undertook the odd bit of M.C'ing at a few of the functions. He gained an enormous amount of personal satisfaction by being part of the group and putting on the shows. It was a great group to be involved in and was certainly a lot of fun.

Fun was a big part of Alf's life, he even ran the men's Pancake Race twice during his life, as well as hosting many Bingo nights locally. Alf had his own special way of calling the numbers which often raised a giggle from those participating.

Later, and having returned from Egypt on active service for nearly 4 years, Alf was employed by Mr. Eaton a Grocer in Midland Road. Grocery life was very different then as to what it is today; produce had to be weighed, packed and priced before it could be delivered. Alf assisted in the shop by taking the orders, serving the customers as well as managing to make deliveries in and around Olney in the shop's grocery van.

Alf had a great love for birds, some of which he bred, and at one time I remember that we had nearly two hundred, give or take a few. Some of them were taken to shows and it was here that Alf made a good deal of friends, some of whom often used to come to him for advice. He was always helping and was very happy doing so, there was always something on the go and it was always interesting with not much time for dull moments.

Mrs Previte

Twenty-five years ago Milton Keynes Social Services Department asked Mrs Vischer of Weston Underwood, who was head of the W.V.S in this area, and who organised the very successful Meals on Wheels Service for Olney and the surrounding area, if the W.V.S would run a Day Centre in Olney.

We had a very successful meeting at Clifton Court with all interested parties and I offered to undertake the job. We were given an initial grant to buy the necessary equipment and a regular quarterly one, as no member should be out of pocket for the food provided and the petrol used. Monday was the most suitable day as the Meals on Wheels were on Tuesdays, Wednesdays and Fridays and the same W.V.S helpers would be involved.

We began with six clients, but the numbers soon grew and we were able to provide them with a good meal, with teas and coffees in the afternoons. We also had knitters which made blankets and coathangers etc and we also hosted a regular Whist Drive. Again the members would collect and take home those that attended and at one time we had over 30 coming from Emberton, Lavendon, Clifton Reynes, Ravenstone, Weston Underwood and Olney.

Over the years things have altered, we are no longer the W.V.S. but we still participate, and with no council grant we now only serve dinner. When we started there was nothing similar in Olney, now of course Age Concern run a Luncheon Club at Clifton Court on Tuesdays and then there is the Kitchener Centre which is very active, and the Community Centre also puts on a lunch on a Thursday.

I retired last autumn having never done anything of a similar nature before, but found it most rewarding and have made many good friends over the years with whom I still keep in touch. I was most fortunate to find a very good successor; Miss Rowledge whose parents both attended the Day Centre.

The late Mrs Barbara Smith

Sadly no longer with us Barbara Smith was Olney's Town Mayor from 2001 - 2003.
During her time with the Diplomatic Service Barbara and her husband Les travelled, lived and worked in several unfamiliar and sometimes hostile countries but despite this any spare time that Barbara had was put to good use; and as well as bringing up a family she managed to obtain several more qualifications along the way. She then went on to master several different languages and even undertook a position translating Braille text books for a school in Kuala Lumpur.

By 1990 Barbara and her husband were back in England and living in Olney and within a short space of time she had taken an active interest in the local community. Eight years later Barbara became President of The Women's Institute in Olney as well as being elected as a member of the Town Council. Within a short space of time she had become Deputy Mayor, and by August 2001 Town Mayor.

Being Olney's Town Mayor was a position that Barbara gave herself wholeheartedly to. She was very much a people's person and she always found the time to stand back and listen to people's concerns and issues. Her duties were always performed with dignity and charm and being such a good listener made her a very effective counsellor and ultimately a great Town Mayor.

At Barbara's funeral sermon on 19th September 2003 the following special reference was made which reflects perfectly how Barbara performed whilst being the Mayor, "Jesus tells us he is a tour courier who has travelled the route before us, who has gone ahead to make sure that the beds are aired, the dinner properly cooked, the beer and wine decently chilled and all the arrangements for our reception are in good order".

A perfect tribute to someone whose contribution to the town will be hard pressed to match and one that will be remembered by many, for many, many years to come.

Captain John Stephen Stewart, O.B.E., F.R.Ag.S.

My grandfather, William Stephen Stewart came to Weston Underwood from Dufftown, Scotland in 1890 to Grange Farm and Peasants Nest Farm. I was born on the 14th July 1922 at Stoneways, Weston Underwood. I was educated at Rushmoor School, Stoke Goldington Rectory, Winchester House, Brackley and Clifton College, Bristol.

I became a medical student, and in 1941 I joined the Royal Marines and served in the Commandos during the war and was wounded three times. However, I was blown up in Cyprus which is when I lost my hearing, so I returned home and farmed with my father at Grange Farm.

My community activities have included the following:

Governor of Carlton Reformatory for 12 years.
Special Constable to Chief Inspector for 10 years.
Formed the Olney Branch of the Arthritis and Rheumatism Council and raised £45,000 in 15 years with them.
National Farmers Union, Chairman of Newport Pagnell, County Chairman on the Council in London for 7 years.
Weston Underwood P.C.C. member and Treasurer for 17 years.

185

Founder and life member of the Northampton branch of International Wine and Food Society, Chairman and Secretary for 17 years.
Country Landowners Association, Member of the County Committee for 7 years.
President of the Northampton branch of Royal Marines Association for 10 years.
General Commissioner for the Inland Revenue for 35 years, Chairman at Milton Keynes for 10 years.
Olney P.C.C. member for 3 years and also their Treasurer.
Secretary of the Newport Pagnell Deanery Church Inspection for 7 years.
Vice President of Olney and District Royal British Legion and President for 5 years, now Secretary.
Director of Nuffield Farming Scholarships Trust for 20 years.
President for 21 years of the Weston Underwood Fishing Club.

Mrs Eileen Mary Stewart

I married John on the 15th July 1954 and was formerly a 3rd Officer in the WRNS.
My community activities include;
Being a member of the Roman Catholic Parish Forum for 3 years.
Co-founder of the Arthritis and Rheumatism Council , as is my husband.
Served 17 years on the Committee of Management at Tickford Abbey WRVS.
Co-founder and life member of the Northampton branch of the International Wine and Food Society.
Hostess to innumerable meetings in connection with other clubs and organisations at Mill House and Netherby House.

The Late Mrs Daphne Tate (nee Barrick)

Sadly no longer with us, Daphne was without a doubt a very popular and well-liked lady within the local community. She was extremely proud of Olney and never tired of helping out wherever she could . She gained much personal satisfaction seeing the progress and development of the clubs, committees and societies that she was involved with within the town.

Daphne held numerous positions of responsibility in the town for many, many years, those being:

Member of the Town Council, 1964-1988
Olney Town Mayor, 1978,1982,1985,1987
Trustee and Chairperson of the Cowper and Newton Museum, Olney.
Chairperson of The Olney Pancake Race Committee.
Founder member of the Olney Floral Fiesta Committee.
Vice President of the Olney Cricket Club.

Committee member for the Ann Hopkins-Smith Charity.
School Governor.

Mr Roy Wilfrid Turner

Was born in Olney and has worked with the community all of his life. Educated originally at Olney Convent, he has on many occasions been guest organist there for weddings, funerals and Christmas Masses. He was the musical director for the funeral of Father Redmond involving 20 priests and the Anglican Church was filled to capacity.

During the 1950s he assisted Eric Kitchener at the Parish Church and has played there on many occasions since. One occasion when the bellows of the Parish Church organ failed, he took his own organ to the church to play for a wedding. He played for the funeral of Mrs Smith, the organist at the Baptist Church and has played there many times since.

He was also pianist for Mrs Suttons dancing classes at what is now The Olney Centre and since 1955 he has been organist at the Cowper Memorial United Reformed Church.

The first ever Floral Fiesta Concert at the Church Hall saw him take his own organ and provide the music there, and has since played and compared a number of Fiesta Talent shows.

Whilst at Reading University he formed the Reading University Operatic Society and directed the first two years productions, and has been rehearsal pianist at some local productions since.

In recent years he has played in thirty six local churches also at Reading, Stowe School and Great Queen Street in London.

As a retailer he has been able to supply many varied and unusual items to the local community and also to many customers in the surrounding districts of Woburn, Bedford and Northampton.

He has been involved with the Senior Citizens gatherings for many years, Children's Christmas Carol Concerts, public charity auctions and has involved his three daughters, son and grandchildren with singing in Olney and around the villages for local causes and parties.

Mrs Valerie Wells

I have been working with children in Olney for over 25 years. It all started when I was a Girl Guide and wanted to help out with my mother's Brownie Pack. As a helper I gained lots of experience and passed my leadership qualifications. When my mother retired from the Brownies in 1990, it seemed natural to me to take over the pack. Brownies really helps girls prepare for later life. I see shy young girls come along to their first meeting and see them leave after 3 years, full of self-confidence and able to work well in group situations, and see them speak confidently with adults. It also gives them a sense of well-being and hopefully, positive thoughts towards their role within the community.

Since starting my own pack 13 years ago, nearly 200 girls have been members, and many of them have been away with me on the annual pack holiday. In 1978 I got an interest in St. John Ambulance. I have worked through different qualifications to enable me to help look after people who have been injured. I have also taken courses in caring for the elderly and sick and I also look after elderly people.

The majority of my work with St. John is helping people who are taken ill or have accidents at events. These events range from Rock Concerts at the Milton Keynes Bowl, local Gymkhana events, the Pancake Race and of course local Rugby games, which is my third passion. Apart from attending organised events, St. John has also given me the skills to help in ad-hoc emergency situations which have helped at two major road accidents.

In 1991 my son wanted to play mini-rugby at Olney. Although Olney has a very strong and mini junior section, there was no specific coach for his under 7 age group. Another dad and I decided that we would run the team. I thought that if I could look after young Brownies then I could look after the young Rugby players. So, when the other dad moved away I took over the coaching of the team. So I could give the boys the best possible coaching I attended the Rugby Football Union's Level 1 coaching course. I also attended a course specifically on scrumageing to ensure that safety aspects in this area are adhered to. I then helped out with my husband at his weekly trainings sessions with the older age group to increase my knowledge of the game. On top of the weekly training, matches and tournaments, I took the whole team to Somerset in 2002 on tour and to play in a competition there, in which we were the runners up.

Rugby is a great game for boys and girls. I have had girls as well as boys play in my team. Rugby allows for children of all different sizes to participate in a great team game, it teaches the young to be part of a team. There are opportunities for individual flare but most of what happens depends on the co-operation of all the players acting together.

The things that I have learnt at St. John Ambulance have been a great help at Rugby. All of the other coaches know that they can call upon me to help with their teams' injuries. I think that Rugby and Brownies help children build friendships that will last a lifetime and also help the children of Olney become better adults who may want to put something back into the community themselves.

Mr Gerald Wilson

Gerald was born on the 13th July 1949 at Emberton and attended schools in both Olney and Emberton. After leaving school he took a job at Pibworth's Farm, Olney as a milkman and later at the age of 17 joined the A.F.S. (Auxiliary Fire Service) and began working with the Green Goddesses. He stayed with the A.F.S for three years until a family crisis struck and he was forced to leave.

Fishing is a much loved and enjoyed hobby of Gerald's, but on one occasion in 1966 whilst at Emberton Gravel Pits, a bad storm quickly blew up and he was struck by lightning, luckily escaping from losing both of his legs.

Gerald has worked in the family business for 35 years starting with delivering coal with his father and grandfather. However in 1987 he was forced to diversify the business and opened a shop at first selling coal, brassware and pet food, thus keeping the family name C.T. Wilson going.

Gerald was asked to re-join the Fire Service and as at July 2003 has managed to complete 33 years as a retained fireman at Olney and is currently Officer-in-Charge. And being a retained member means that you are on call 24 hours a day, 7 days per week. His life has revolved around the Fire Service and there have been numerous occasions when many locals have been pleased to see him. However, in December 2004 he will retire after serving the community for 35 years.

St. John Ambulance has also played a big part in his life. 4 out of 5 children have all been members, and when the family was younger he was on the committee formed to raise money for the group, the outings, social evenings and race nights.

He is now Captain of the Outdoor Bowls Club here in Olney and Captain of Bridgman's Indoor Club, Harrold and is also a member of the Olney Chamber of Trade.

Olney's Past Community Workers

Samuel Teedon

Samuel Teedon came to Olney from Bedford in 1775 and lived in a small cottage just off the High Street, earning a pittance as a teacher. It was here that he lived with his cousin Elizabeth Killingsworth, her son Eusebius and Polly Taylor whom he often referred to as his daughter. Seventeen years later, from October 1791 to February 1794, Samuel decided to keep a personal account / record of his life whilst living in Olney.

Samuel was a regular acquaintance of William Cowper and Mrs Unwin and his journal, which contains many references to them, is one of the reasons why this gentleman's diary has become an important link with Olney's past.
Samuel also corresponded a great deal with Cowper and Mrs Unwin, in fact records show,

72	letters from William Cowper to Samuel
17	letters from Mrs Unwin to Samuel
126	letters from Samuel to William Cowper
62	letters from Samuel to Mrs Unwin

William Cowper considered Samuel a bit of a bore (which Samuel seemed unaware of) and yet also appeared to be amused by him, which can be seen in a letter dated 25th February 1781 to the Reverend John Newton,

"He has just left us after a long visit the greatest part of which he spent in the narration of certain detail of facts that might have been compressed into a much smaller compass".

Nevertheless, William Cowper and Mrs Unwin must have taken pity on Samuel because they frequently relieved his poverty with financial assistance.

Samuel was a well-educated man of the church. He knew his New Testament thoroughly and could read it in both Greek and Latin. He also took an interest in French, in addition to being passionate about English literature. He earned his living by teaching and, with the assistance of Eusebius; he ran a school in Sheil Hall, a curious building which stood on the Market Place. Eusebius had many talents, as well as being a bookbinder he was also a penman, arithmetician and algebraist. Sadly their work was not appreciated and as a result they remained very poor. (Some teachers of today might say that nothing has changed!)

Early in June 1794, Samuel died after a night's illness and was buried in Olney's churchyard on 9th June 1794. After his death, his diary was passed to the Johnson family for safekeeping but it disappeared for some years, only to be re-discovered by Mr W J Harvey. Mr Harvey eventually passed this small book, measuring 6" x 3 3/4 " and containing 122 pages of neatly handwritten text, to Mr W H Collingbridge, the originator of the Cowper and Newton Museum.

On the 25th April 1900, (the centenary of William Cowper's death) Mr Collingbridge presented the diary to the Museum at the same time as he bequeathed Orchard Side to the people of Olney.

Some time after Samuels's death William Soul, a lace designer in Olney, wrote a manuscript about Samuel's life and also a diary. William, who died on Friday 3rd March 1865, was described as "an intelligent and thoughtful man, who was something of an artist and something of a poet".

In 1902 Thomas Wright, by then Curator of the Museum, took a closer look at the diary and found that Samuel, God bless him, was a bit erratic with his spelling and grammar. He therefore embarked upon correcting it and then translating it into a more legible and presentable format. This work also made it easier to identify the characters to whom Samuel was referring.

Thus one man's diary became two and they are both in the possession of the Cowper and Newton Museum.

Joseph Garner

Joseph G Garner set up business on the east side of the Market Place trading as " Garners Drapers, Outfitters and Furnishing Store" which had the longest shop front in the Town.

Joseph was born in Newport Pagnell and was educated there at the British School. In 1877 he forfeited his free, three-year scholarship for further education to enter the world of business, at the young age of 12.

His first job was in a printers but he later moved on to a drapers, where he stayed for 6 years, watching and learning the secrets and tricks of the trade. This stood him in good stead for he eventually left and moved to Olney, opening his own business there around 1886.

Joseph very quickly became a well-liked and respected trader in Olney and on the 31st May 1893 he married a Miss Davies and settled down with her in Olney. He would often recall his early days in Olney, when there was no Midland Road, no factory, no electric lighting, no sanitary arrangements, scarcely any fresh water and all the streets were cobbled.

Joseph took a keen interest in the Town and participated in many of Olney's activities. He was also a devout Christian and a prominent member of the Congregational Church in the High Street, where as a lay preacher he often took the services when the pastor was absent and was also the Church's Sunday school teacher.

Among other things Joseph was a leading light with the Museum and became Curator and a Trustee. This was a position he thoroughly enjoyed and he regularly took groups of visitors on guided tours around the house.

When Joseph died in 1944 after a long illness, the whole Town mourned his loss but his business continued trading successfully in the hands of his son Tom.

In 1970 the business closed and the shop was divided into smaller units. When Tom died he left a small legacy to the Town Council with no stipulation how it should be spent but the money went towards improvements and alterations to the Market Place.

Not forgetting to mention the Chairmen and Mayors of Olney

1894 - 1895	Archibald Allen	
1895 - 1896	John Charles Hipwell	
1896 - 1898	William Clarabut	
1898 - 1899	John Whitmee	
1899 - 1901	George William Field	
1901 - 1913	John William Mann	
1913 - 1919	John Whitmee	Chairmen of the Council
1919 - 1922	John Lord	
1922 - 1931	William Edward Pebody	
1931 - 1934	Charles Mortimer Allen	
1934 - 1937	Albert John Wiffen	
1937 - 1952	Stanley W. Lord	
1952 -	Albert George Morgan	
1953 - 1973	Leslie Ernest Fairey	
1973 - 1978	Nigel Denns Vincent Swallow	1st Mayor
1978 - 1882	Daphne Freda Barrick	
1982 - 1983	William Gilbert Pebody	
1983 - 1984	Geoffrey Morgan	
1984 - 1985	Leonard Alfred Dix	
1985 - 1987	Daphne Freda Tate	
1987 -	Eric Dodworth	
1987 - 1990	John Richard Boardman	
1990 - 1994	Anthony William Evans	
1994 - 1998	Deirdre Bethune	
1998 - 2002	David M Price	
2002 - 2003	Barbara Smith	
2003 -	Sallyann Rogers	

Information taken from Room 3, Olney Centre

Bibliography

Romance of the Lace Pillow, Thomas Wright
Lace Our Heritage, Madeline Van Horrik
A Lace Walk around Olney, Cowper & Newton Museum
Olney Past & Present, Ratcliff and Brown, 1893
Victorian Transport Schemes, 1863- 1900, Gerald Mann, 1996
Collins Latin Dictionary, Harper Collins, 1996
The Domesday Book, England's Heritage Then and Now, Coombe Books, 1996
The Domesday Book, A Complete Translation, Penguin, 2002
From Romans to Roundabouts, C. R. Perkins
History & Topography of Buckinghamshire
The Newport Hundreds
A Companion to the Folklore Myths and Customs of Britain, Marc Alexander, Sutton Publishing, 2002
The Soul Family of Olney, Buckinghamshire Soul Search, Bob Solly, March 1997
The Olney Fire Ballads, Gordon Osborne, Cowper & Newton Museum
The Diary of Samuel Teedon, Thomas Wright, 1902
Memories of Buckinghamshire Picture Palaces, Martin Tapsell, Mercia Cinema Publications Group
The Buildings of England, Buckinghamshire, Nikolaus Pevsner, Penguin Books, 1960
The Fires of Olney, a Mystery Explained, J. Taylor

Recommended Local books

All of which can be found in the local library or purchased from Words Bookshop, High Street South, Olney.

The Old Inns of Olney, Elizabeth Knight, Barracuda Books Ltd, 1981
The Olney Millennium Almanac, Reflections on Life in Olney, 1900-2000,Olney & District Historical Society, 2000
Reminiscences of Life in and around Olney, Olney & District Historical Society, 2002
The Story of the Olney Pancake Race, Graham Lenton, GML Art, 2003
Images of England, Around Olney, Joan Jones, Tempus Publishing, 2003

Many thanks

Mr Bob and Mrs Dorothy Soul and family
Mr Tony Ockenden
Mr Mark Covington
Mr Gerald Mann
Mrs Karen Parr, Cowper and Newton Museum Olney
Mrs Mona Morgan
The Rev. Nigel Pond
Mr Martin Edwards
Mrs Betty Pibworth
Mr Peter and Mrs Ruth Revitt
Dr Graham Lenton
Sites and Monuments Office Milton Keynes
Olney Clutch Club
The various ladies at the County Records Office, Aylesbury